Small Libraries, Big Impact

SMALL LIBRARIES, BIG IMPACT

How to Better Serve Your Community in the Digital Age

Yunfei Du

Foreword by
Hon. Robert S. Martin, PhD

LIBRARIES UNLIMITED™

An Imprint of ABC-CLIO, LLC

Santa Barbara, California • Denver, Colorado

Library of Congress Cataloging-in-Publication Data

Names: Du, Yunfei, 1970- author.
Title: Small libraries, big impact : how to better serve your community in the digital age / Yunfei Du.
Description: Santa Barbara, CA : Libraries Unlimited, [2016] | Includes bibliographical references and index.
Identifiers: LCCN 2015049681 (print) | LCCN 2016017929 (ebook) | ISBN 9781440841569 (paperback) | ISBN 9781440841576 (ebook)
Subjects: LCSH: Libraries and community—United States. | Library outreach programs—United States. | Public libraries—Social aspects—United States. | Small libraries—United States—Case studies. | Rural libraries—United States—Case studies.
Classification: LCC Z716.4 .D82 2016 (print) | LCC Z716.4 (ebook) | DDC 027.473—dc23
LC record available at https://lccn.loc.gov/2015049681

ISBN: 978-1-4408-4156-9
EISBN: 978-1-4408-4157-6

20 19 18 17 16   1 2 3 4 5

This book is also available on the World Wide Web as an eBook.
Visit www.abc-clio.com for details.

Libraries Unlimited
An Imprint of ABC-CLIO, LLC

ABC-CLIO, LLC
130 Cremona Drive, P.O. Box 1911
Santa Barbara, California 93116-1911

This book is printed on acid-free paper ∞

Manufactured in the United States of America

CONTENTS

FOREWORD

Public libraries in the United States are indispensable institutions. There are more public libraries in the United States than there are McDonald's restaurants—16,604 library service outlets compared with 14,339 McDonald's restaurants (Columbus Public Library, 2015). In the past decade, two-thirds of Americans annually visited a public library at least once, and 62% of adults in the United States had public library cards (American Library Association, 2015a). In 2012, there were 1.5 billion in-person visits to public libraries across the United States—a 10-year increase of 20.7% (American Library Association, 2015b). And Americans love their libraries: according to a recent Pew Research Center report, 90% of Americans ages 16 and older say that the closing of their local public library would have an adverse impact on their community (Pew Research Center, 2014). These statistics state the obvious: the American public library is a heavily used and ubiquitous institution.

The 16,536 public library outlets in the United States are administered by 9,041 separate library systems. Of these systems, 7,321—or 80%—are single outlet libraries (American Library Association, 2015a). These libraries primarily serve small and rural communities. Because 80% of public library systems serve towns with populations less than 25,000, this is especially true in small town America. Rare is the small town without a public library. In the past century, thousands of small public libraries have circulated billions of books to citizens. More important, they have also served as destinations, places where citizens can go to learn, to become informed, and to create community.

In his book *Main Street Public Library*, historian Wayne A. Wiegand demonstrated the impact that small town public libraries have on their communities. Wiegand documented that the primary purpose and mission of small town libraries "was to foster the kinds of social harmony that community spaces and stories—experienced and shared—provide" (Wiegand, 2011, p. 186). Main Street Libraries served primarily as a civic space for the creation of social cohesion and reinforcement of local values and taste, defining for each community what Wiegand terms a "uniquely negotiated cultural center" (Wiegand, 2011, p. 183).

But as Professor Du demonstrates in detail in the pages that follow, rural libraries face significant challenges. They are small and often isolated, and they compete for a limited pool of local resources. Funding for rural libraries is overwhelmingly local: four-fifths of all rural public library expenditures come from local sources, primarily local ad-valorem and sales tax revenue. To secure operating resources, rural public libraries must compete with other highly valued services, including police and fire protection, public schools, and even sanitation.

Urban Libraries Council (2011, p. 1) suggested the importance of public libraries providing highly valued services to communities:

> Research and experience demonstrate that engaged and empowered citizens generate optimism about the future, produce good decisions on tough community challenges, and contribute to economic success and individual well-being. Public libraries, with their sustained stature as the most trusted government entity, are ideal resources to shape and lead discussions, decisions, and strategies that encourage active and purposeful civic engagement. Yet, despite the assets, resources, and experience that libraries bring to the table, they are rarely seen as community and civic engagement leaders.

Too often libraries are viewed by local government officials and resource allocators as nice things to have when we can afford them. "Failing to leverage the library's broad community connections, respected public stature, and capacity to bring people together is a missed opportunity" (Urban Libraries Council, 2011, p. 1).

To help address this situation, and empower one segment of the rural public library sector, in 2010, the University of North Texas's College of Information initiated a three-year project, funded by a $1.6 million grant from the Robert and Ruby Priddy Charitable Trust. The project was given the name **P**romoting & **E**nhancing the **A**dvancement of **R**ural **L**ibraries (PEARL) (University of North Texas, 2010). The PEARL project was designed to strengthen the public library as an essential part of community life in rural communities in Texas. The idea behind the PEARL project was to change the perception of libraries, from role players to valued leaders in today's civic engagement space, and achieve recognition of the public library as an *essential* service, just like the police and fire departments and the local schools (Blake, Martin, & Du, 2011, p. 2).

The purpose of the project was not to try to tell the participants what to do, or to invent their library services program from scratch. Most of the librarians in small and rural communities are very capable. They have deep roots in their communities. They generally know the people, their needs and concerns, and the issues that command attention. They already provide important resources and services. The purpose of the PEARL project was to assist them in strengthening their ability to demonstrate the value of the library and develop partners in the community. The approach was to provide them with a set of tools and a process to achieve that end. Ultimately, we expected to help them change the public perception of the library in the community from a *nicety* to a *necessity*.

The success of the PEARL project underscores that the approach we took can be extended more generally to all public libraries. The underlying principle of our approach was the necessity to demonstrate public value. Library public value is determined by users.

> In a sense, really, this is a no-brainer: if public enterprises do not create value for the public, then why would they be formed or continue to exist? The problem, of course, is how do you define and measure public value?
>
> A key concept in determining public value is that value is determined not by the providers of services, but the consumers. In other words, we don't decide what is valuable, our users or customers do. If we want to offer services that the public will value and support, it is imperative that we *listen* carefully and systematically to our elected officials and resource allocators to understand fully their agendas, their concerns, and their goals. (Martin, 2003, p. 4)

We need then to take care to explain how libraries can help library users achieve *their* goals and advance *their* agendas.

This is essentially a marketing approach. A simple definition of marketing is that it consists of asking a group or an individual what product or service they want to buy or support and then developing a product or service that meets the identified demand (http://www.imls.gov/whatsnew/current/sp040103.htm).

So in order to demonstrate value and secure the support we need in our communities, we must engage in real marketing. We need to use marketing tools like focus groups and surveys to provide structured ways to listen to the communities we seek to serve. And we need to ask them not about what we do that they like and don't like. We need instead to pursue truly deep inquiries into what they want and need to make their lives better. And then we need to fashion programs and services that meet those needs and desires. For example, it is far less important to ask users what hours they want the library to be open than it is to ask them what their goals and needs are and then think creatively about what we can do to help them achieve their goals or fulfill their needs. Ask them what the issues in their daily lives that they care most about are and then respond appropriately (http://www.imls.gov/whatsnew/current/sp040503.htm).

Professor Du provides a detailed description and analysis of the kind of community outreach that is required to create sustained support for the services that public libraries provide. These efforts often involve establishing partnerships with other entities in the community. These kind of collaborative efforts can strengthen the library's ability to provide needed programs and services and to encourage library use by those who heretofore had not darkened the library's door. Listening to our communities provides a framework for identifying trends that affect our perceived value in the community and allow libraries to take early steps to address shifts in those perceptions.

It is imperative that we examine the place of the library in its social context. This volume offers a thorough discussion of the relevance of social justice initiatives and social inclusion, emphasizing the need to reach out to disengaged segments of the community, including low-income families and the homeless, seniors, immigrants, and those for whom English is a second language, as well as those most impacted by the digital divide. Real-world examples of successful approaches are provided.

The role of libraries as information anchors in their communities has not been overlooked. Especially in rural areas, where broadband connectivity is often expensive or even lacking entirely, libraries act as an effective lifeline to the digital world. Whether Internet access is used to search for employment opportunities, to locate sources of information for handling important personal challenges like medical conditions or legal entanglements, or simply to connect to sources of entertainment and enrichment, the library is an indispensable resource. The function of this service alone can demonstrate extraordinary value to the community.

The volume that follows is a comprehensive treatment of the challenges faced by all public libraries, but especially those libraries serving small and rural communities. It provides conceptual and practical tools for serving diverse users, gaining wide community support, programming dynamic events, and planning rewarding technology learning spaces in libraries. Properly employed, this text offers an engaging strategy for library managers to demonstrate successfully the public value that their agencies provide, cement their standing in the communities that they serve, and truly empower the big impact that they make.

Hon. Robert S. Martin, PhD
Lillian Bradshaw Professor Emeritus
Texas Woman's University

REFERENCES

American Library Association. (2015a). *Number of libraries in the United States.* Chicago, IL: American Library Association. Available at http://www.ala.org/tools/libfactsheets/alalibraryfactsheet01

American Library Association. (2015b). *Public library use.* Chicago, IL: American Library Association. Available at http://www.ala.org/tools/libfactsheets/alalibraryfactsheet06

Blake, B., Martin, R. S., & Du, Y. (2011). *Successful community outreach: A how-to-do-it manual for librarians.* New York: Neal-Schuman.

Columbus Public Library. (2015). *Library Connection,* 2(7). Available at http://www.columbusne.us/Archive/ViewFile/Item/881

Martin, R. (2003). *Keeping good company: A vindication of collaboration.* Paper presented at 2003 Symposium of Philadelphia Area Consortium of Special Collections Libraries. Available at http://archives.pacscl.org/news/2003/symposium/martin.pdf

Pew Research Center. (2014). *From distant admirers to library lovers—and beyond. A typology of library engagement in America.* Washington, DC: Pew Research Center. Available at http://www.pewinternet.org/2014/03/13/library-engagement-typology/

University of North Texas. (2010). *UNT receives grant to assist rural libraries.* Denton, TX: University of North Texas. Available at http://pearl.unt.edu/unt-received-grant -assist-rural-libraries

Urban Libraries Council. (2011). *Library priority: Community-civic engagement.* Urban Libraries Council Leadership Brief. Washington, DC: Urban Libraries Council. Available at http://www.nlc.org/documents/Find%20City%20Solutions/Research%20 Innovation/Governance-Civic/library-priority-community-civic-engagement-fall11.pdf

Wiegand, W. A. (2011). *Main street public library: Community places and reading spaces in the rural heartland, 1876–1956.* Iowa City, IA: University of Iowa Press.

CHAPTER ONE

Libraries, Users, and Communities: An Introduction

The library has a long history as a place to store, organize, and process human knowledge. However, libraries were not open to the public until the 18th century in Europe when the subscription library emerged. Subscription library use was restricted to members, and these libraries were supported by annual fees or by the selling of shares to members (Kelly, 1966).

When settling North America, colonists from England brought along their own personal collections and started fee-based libraries. By the mid-17th century, colonists had established libraries that local community members could access. Benjamin Franklin established the Library Company of Philadelphia in 1731 and founded the first social libraries (Richards, Wiegand, & Dalbello, 2015). Social libraries allowed anybody to use the library through either a fee or a subscription or through classification of the person as a co-owner or as a stockholder of the library (Davis & Tucker, 1989, p. 56; McMullen, 2000, p. 63). Colonial America also saw the emergence of circulating libraries, a model of library in which collections were rented to any customer for a fee.

While social and circulating libraries experienced moderate success, on November 20, 1790, in Franklin, Massachusetts, there was a town hall meeting in which a vote was held to allow every resident the ability to use the books in the library for free. This established the first public library in the United States (http://www.town.franklin.ma.us/Pages/FranklinMA_Library/libraryhistory). The 19th century also witnessed the founding of the American Library Association (ALA) and its journal, which were both heavily promoted by Melvil Dewey. Tax-supported public libraries were first established successfully in America, and they reflected the philosophy that a library should be funded by the community and accessed freely by all community users. In addition to tax support, generous philanthropists also played a major role in establishing both public and academic libraries.

Andrew Carnegie, the American steel magnate and philanthropist, donated a considerable amount of his fortune to charities and libraries, both academic and public, for their buildings and collections. Carnegie believed public libraries were as essential to the development of citizens as elementary education (Bobinski, 1969, p. 183). Following the model of Carnegie libraries, funding from private parties began to support small towns and communities in establishing their own libraries, and many such small libraries continue to serve community users today (p. 199). Libraries, regardless of size, are built on the idea of meeting the interests and needs of the patrons. In 1931, Ranganathan summarized five laws of libraries: books are for use; every reader has his/her book; every book has its reader; save the time of the reader; and the library is a growing organism. It is a principle of practice that a library should be centered on its users, particularly that library collections should meet the special interests of the community, and that libraries should promote and advertise their services extensively in order to attract a wide range of readers (Ranganathan & Gopinath, 1966; Dayal, 2011).

This chapter serves as an overview of the concept of libraries and the development of libraries into the digital era: the funding, the understanding of diverse users, the collection, the library as an educational opportunity, the library as an access point to digital resources, the qualities needed for the director, and the community factors.

FUNDING FOR SMALL AND RURAL LIBRARIES

American public libraries are largely supported by local sources. According to the ALA (2014), in the fiscal year 2012, an estimated 84.4% of public libraries' total operating revenue of $11.5 billion came from local sources; 6.9% from state sources; 0.5% from federal sources; and 8.2% from other sources, including monetary gifts and donations, interest, library fines, fees for library services, and grants (Institute of Museum and Library Services, 2013). ALA research on library funding concluded that at the federal budget level, "many other programs that benefit libraries have been severely cut or in some cases terminated" (http://www.ala.org/advocacy/libfunding/fed). When 84.4% of operating revenues comes from local funding, for public libraries, especially rural public libraries, securing local funding must be their focus to survive.

A study by the Institute of Museum and Library Services (IMLS) (2013) reported most public library revenues typically come from local government sources. In the fiscal year 2011, rural libraries received 80.2% of their total revenue from local government sources and 10.3% from state governments, an increase of 4.5% in local revenue and a decrease of 20.4% in state revenue over the past three year period. It is noteworthy that some libraries in poor rural communities are in survival mode. They must compete with other city or county departments, such as fire and police, for budget allocation. If there is a revenue shortfall, the library budget is often the first to be cut.

IMLS (2013) reported that public libraries in the United States spent 65.4% of their collection budget on print materials and 14.3% on electronic resources such as e-books, e-serials, government documents, and software. Other formats such as microform, audio, video, and DVDs accounted for 20.4%. The decision to develop various types of items within a library collection is determined by users' interest. But where does the money come from, what are the "local sources," and who awards the funds to buy these resources?

Local Funding

As the statistics revealed, funding for rural and small public libraries mainly comes from local sources, which may include city or county tax support, private donations, local foundations, and endowments. The practice of funding public libraries with city or county tax support is to promote education. Public education is no good if "it awakens a taste for reading, but it furnishes to the public nothing to be read" (Augst & Wiegand, 2003, p. 10). The public library is an agency that can encourage learning and a taste for reading. It can promote social independence rather than social welfare.

Foundations and private donors recognized the impact of libraries, and many have been supporting libraries for years or even decades. The Bill & Melinda Gates Foundation, for example, has provided funding for public access computers, Internet access, and access to digital information to low-income communities (Riva, 2001). Although the Gates Foundation is gradually moving out of funding libraries, the resources and staff training it provided are valuable assets for library services (Chant, 2014).

While local private donations, endowments, and grants can cover some costs, the money is usually restricted to starting an initiative, improving the physical building, developing a collection, or enhancing technologies and is rarely used to fund operating costs, such as staff salaries and utilities. When there is a reduced expenditure allocation, often the first expense to be cut in the budget is materials for the collection. Local charities and private resources can help sustain the libraries during a time of emergency budget cuts, but in the long run, libraries need to be fully supported by the city or county government funding. These funds are backed by income or property taxes, and the amount can fluctuate severely year to year. For example, in the ALA 2011–2012 *Public Library Funding Landscape* report, it stated, "Rural libraries continue to make double-digit reductions in collections (e.g., the highest cuts reported are between -33.9 percent and -45.4 percent), reallocating funds to other expenditure categories." (http://www.ala.org/research/sites/ala.org.research/files/content/initiatives/plftas/2011_2012/plftas12_funding%20landscape.pdf, American Library Association, 2012, p. 11)

To maintain stable funding support, small public libraries need to demonstrate their value to their city or county officials, advisory board, or other governing entities.

City or County Council (Government) Funding

Libraries within cities or counties report to the governing body of that entity such as a city council, city management, or the county commissioners. Many public libraries are part of the local government and are supported by tax revenues, but city or county funding may not always be sufficient, especially in difficult economic times. As property tax makes up a large portion of revenue for cities and counties, the demographics of a community may greatly impact a library's community support, and small cities with fewer residents can be impacted more harshly by an economic downtown.

In time of economic hardship, without sufficient funding, material purchases will be cut first, followed by staff positions or work time. Kelley (2012) wrote a report on library budget surveys in 2012:

> "The worst impact on the library in terms of budget cuts are in the area of staffing," said one librarian at a small library in Illinois. "We are constantly short-staffed and must do the work of two librarians at all times. This is our new normal."
>
> A full 78 percent of the survey respondents said that in order to cope with staff cuts (77 percent of which came through attrition or a hiring freeze) they had to absorb a greater workload and be cross-trained.

To secure more funding opportunities, libraries need to demonstrate to social leaders including elected officers and resource allocators in their community that the value and services libraries offer are considered to be inseparable from the community.

Library Board Funding

Some community libraries are founded by private funds and have since evolved as nonprofit organizations. A library running as a nonprofit organization (501c3) needs to have an advisory board, for tax purposes, and each state may have its own guidelines for library the advisory board requirements. The success of a small library is largely dependent on how well its advisory board advocates for library support, including financial support for annual or operational and capital funding (Todaro, 2012, p. 7). The library director may apply for special funding support to the advisory board that may raise funds from communities in order to support a special project that will benefit the library.

As mentioned before, public libraries support both the informal and the formal lifelong learning of diverse community residents. Many individuals committed to the process, and results show that, through offering library services to the public, these residents have become members and officers of library boards, friends, and volunteer groups in order to show their support and attempt to better the libraries within their community.

UNDERSTANDING DIVERSE USERS IN LIBRARIES

Public libraries in North America revolve around the philosophy that all individuals, regardless of age or race, should have access to the resources available through the libraries, which coincides with the growth of diverse populations of America, as a distinguishing characteristic of the American society is its diverse population.

Ever since the founding of the New World, the American population has been vastly diverse both ethnically and culturally. The United States Census (2013) reported that, among the 318 million people, 62.6% are white, not Hispanic or Latino; 17.1% are Hispanic or Latino; 13.2% are black or African American; 5.3% are Asian; 1.2% are American Indian and Alaska Native; and 2.4% are two or more races (http://quickfacts.census.gov/qfd/states/00000.html). Census data (2008) also showed that the country is just as diverse regarding religion, as of the 228 million adults in the population, 76% are Christians, 3.9% are among other religions, and 14.9% do not have a religion specified. Among Christians, there are Baptists (25%), Lutherans (4.9%), Presbyterians (7.3%), Protestants—nondenominational (15.8%), and Christians—no denomination (7.4%). Among other religions, there are Jewish, Muslim, Buddhist, Hindu, and so on (United States Census, 2008).

The 2010 Census also shows that the foreign-born population is distributed unevenly, with 53% from Latin America, 28% from Asia, 12% from Europe, and 5% from other countries. The top five birth countries comprising this foreign-born population are Mexico (11.7 million), China (2.2 million), India (1.8 million), and Vietnam (1.2 million) (United States Census, 2010).

Traditionally, the concept of user diversity refers to people from different cultural and ethnic backgrounds, but Peterson (1999) reviewed the concept of diversity in the United States Civil Rights Act of 1964, which is rooted in equity, equality, and affirmative action, and concluded that opportunity must also be included. She wrote:

> With the passage and signing of the Civil Rights Acts of 1964, which dismantled the discretionary laws directed at African Americans, it was recognized that abolishing the laws was not enough. Opportunity needed to be provided as well. By an executive order in 1965, the phase Affirmative Action was added to our lexicon. This phase was grounded in civil rights, equity, and justice, whereas diversity is grounded only in difference. (p. 19)

The focus of library service has been and will continue to be its users, but unfortunately until now libraries have a long history of "reaching out" to users in the means of "handing out the same old wares in a different way" (Boyce & Boyce, 1995). The profession now requires library managers to perform a broad spectrum of activities and to better serve diverse users. The concept of diversity needs to be expanded in our digital age as it has a direct relationship to what is placed in the library collection.

Diversity has a new meaning these days. Due to various levels of technological backgrounds, community incomes, and infrastructure, even with same ethnic group, users may have different level of access to the Internet, including its contained technologies, and digital resources. Compared with urban or suburban towns, information technology and communication infrastructure in rural cities and communities can be more expensive to install and less robust and reliable, thus depriving different ethnic groups of access to the Internet.

In addition to different income levels, sexual orientation and gender identity are other topics of interests in library and information science literature. ALA promotes the equality of user services through its profession and has an active round table on gay, lesbian, bisexual, and transgender (GLBT) services, promoting book awards, conference programs, and professional tools to these diverse communities.

Mehra and Braquet (2007) discussed the information needs of GLBT individuals and proposed that the support services offered by library and information science (LIS) professionals can meet various information needs as well as provide social justice. The services can be conceptual tools used to represent and advocate diverse users, promote outreach and community building, and provide effective information dissemination to all community users.

This book defines diversity in library services as different levels of cultural backgrounds, ethnicities, technology backgrounds, income levels, gender identities, and technological facilities. Chapter 5 will discuss in detail serving diverse users in library services.

BOOKS AND BYTES IN LIBRARIES

Collections have been the foundation of library and information services, and today librarians constantly need to develop and manage their collections to satisfy their users and facilitate lifelong learning by enhancing the materials, which include print books or e-books, DVDs, journals, and magazines. At the same time, librarians must provide various user services to ensure that all users have access to print or digital resources. Many librarians increasingly spend resources on electronic databases, e-books, and other forms of electronic information delivery to its users; they also promote and train the community on the use of digital resources, including e-books, and e-readers. However, in many rural and small libraries, traditional print resources are still popular among the users, partially due to the lack of access to digital resources.

Evans and Zarnosky (2000) suggested that the philosophy of building a library's collection is to meet the information needs of the community that the collection serves (p. 17). Also, in her book, Johnson (2009, p. 129) stated:

> Diverse collections address and respond to the needs and interests of an increasingly diverse society, including individuals with disabilities; single parent and

other nontraditional families; gay, lesbian, bisexual, and transgender individuals; and foreign born and nonnative English speakers.

Not only do users come to the library building to pick up print books for reading for pleasure, they also now come to use library computers and technology spaces or to attend children's programs and other services offered to users. However, collections and services offered by libraries come with a cost, and many users may not realize that libraries need to have a reliable income in order to fund book purchases, journal subscriptions, databases, and technologies, as well as to provide the needed services and management of daily operations, maintenance, and personnel cost. This lack of understanding regarding the costs of providing "free" library services has various reasons and is particularly noted by those people who are just becoming eligible to vote in elections and for those interested in the bonds issued to support libraries. And in order to include as many diversity-promoting resources as possible, even greater costs are incurred. Naidoo (2014) suggested that the diversity found in library collections and programs is essentially cultural diversity, and "culture includes shared characteristics that define how a person lives, thinks, and creates meaning. These characteristics include customs, traditions, rituals, food, dress, and language" (p. 2). In addition, a person's cultural background also include factors such as race, family origin, physical ability, sexual orientation, income and socioeconomic status, language competency, immigration status, religion, age, and gender. If a library's print or digital collection does not include a user's cultural background, it sends a message to certain users that their librarian does not think they are important enough to feature in the library. Such lack of representation could even be harmful to a patron's self-image. Library researchers have a long tradition of understanding diversity needed in collections in order to help to build better communities. For example, Totten, Garner, and Brown (1996) created a guideline of how to develop culture-oriented library collections in libraries, and the principle is still very important in building today's digital or nonprint collections, such as DVDs, games, and software packages, which are the materials that attract many community users to a library today.

Age as a Factor in Collection Building

The age groups of the users a library serves is an important factor in library collection building. Young people and senior citizens may have different reading interests.

Young People

Age plays an important role when dividing different levels of Internet users. Young people are often called "digital natives," and Krotoski (2011) commented that young people are often constantly on the Internet, constantly promoting themselves, and constantly connected. She also concluded that young age is a period of self-expression, and young people frequently use social network tools and communicate with peers going through the similar physical, psychological, and social changes. At the same time, older patrons are digital immigrants who might be eager to learn new technologies but need to constantly and quickly adapt to new environments that are not in their comfort zones. Therefore, a library needs to provide various programs to accommodate a broad prospective of different users.

The Benton Foundation (1997) suggested that young Americans between the ages of 18 and 24 are less interested in maintaining library buildings, and they are also the least enthusiastic of any age group considering the roles of libraries in a digital era. They prefer to spend the resources on personal computers rather than on tax support to the library for acquiring digital information resources. If this age group does not use the library, there is a chance that the library will eventually lose revenue distributions to other governmental agencies in the community. While this is a concern for libraries of all sizes, librarians in small and rural libraries especially need to focus on providing services for this age group within their communities.

Older Users

Something that affects both young and old users of the library is the ability to gain access to its resources. However, library users must be able to access the new resources, specifically digital, and this could be a challenge for older users, as they may be reluctant to try new technologies with which they are not familiar. Zickuhr, Purcell, and Rainie (2014) categorized all library users into three engagement groups, those being high engagement, medium engagement, and low engagement. One of the low engagement groups consists of those considered to be the "rooted and road blocked" residents; this is the most senior group and comprises a large number of retirees. A majority of them have low Internet usage (74%), home broadband coverage (58%), smartphone ownership (40%), and social media use. Many people from this group also feel less comfortable with tasks that are related to technologies.

In addition, regardless of their level of technical savvy, some older adults may not speak English as their first language and may struggle to read in English. Since most resources in a library, both printed books and digital, require reading knowledge, people with reading or language challenges, either physical or technical, will have difficulty in making use of the library's resources.

Competition in the Community as a Factor in Collection Building

The same research conducted is also concerned that functions of libraries in larger cities face competition from bookstores such as Barnes and Noble because "not only did these stores have popular books in stock (something libraries fell down on), but they created a welcoming atmosphere with comfortable chairs, coffee, and music playing in the background." (Benton Foundation, 1997, p. 182).

While most small towns and rural areas do not have bookstores, they must use the example of what makes a bookstore popular (a comfortable environment) to make their libraries more appealing to users. Even with limited funding, rural public libraries serve as community centers where residents can check out print or digital books, socialize, and use the free Internet for various reasons, including lifelong learning.

Understanding the Information Needs of Diverse Users

To make the library an essential part of the community and to secure library funding from various avenues, it is logical for librarians to understand the information needs of their diverse user groups so that they can better justify their roles to local government and promote their services to various local residents.

Case (2012, p. 84) reviewed the concept and models of information needs and cited Dervin's model of information needs. Dervin (1992) explained the concept of information need as a situation in which there is an information gap that needs to be filled. The gap exists when one asks questions in order to make sense of his/her situation. For rural libraries serving diverse users, it seems more relevant to define human information needs using Maslow's (1968) model, which includes five levels of needs: physiological needs, safety needs, belongingness needs, esteem needs, and self-actualization needs, all of which can be applied to different kinds of user groups.

Libraries need to accommodate all kinds of diverse users within their communities, but special attention must be given to the distinction between immigrant and nonimmigrant user groups. Immigrants include people who are foreign born and most often speak English as a second language. Shoham and Strauss (2008) believed that for immigrants, the concept of immigration is the gap, with subneeds being housing, education, transportation, medical issues, legal issues, work, language, and so forth. Similarly, nonimmigrant residents may be a different gender, ethnicity, or age and have different income levels that precipitate different information needs and information gaps; these gaps require that different amounts of attention be given to the different levels of need: physiological, safety, belongingness, esteem, and self-actualization.

LIBRARY AS EDUCATIONAL OPPORTUNITY

Traditionally, public libraries have provided information access and educational opportunities free for all people, regardless of their ethnic background and socioeconomic status, and this is still true today of rural libraries. The cost of education continues to rise, and researchers Edwards, Rauseo, and Unger (2013) emphasized the concept of the library's role as needing to be the "people's universities," especially as residents in rural areas have less access to the resources that are found in larger cities and universities. However, access to digital and online resources to expand the print collections has helped to overcome some of this need.

Rural libraries have abundant online training opportunities to provide literacy training to their communities. For example, WebJunction and the Association for Rural and Small Libraries hosted a webinar by Debra A. Kavanaugh, of the Shreve Memorial Library, on how small and rural libraries provide important and successful adult education programs for patrons without General Educational Development (GED), or other high school equivalency (http://www .webjunction.org/events/webjunction/crafting-a-successful-adult-education -program.html). Rural libraries have the potential to provide various training opportunities on literacy and digital technologies in their communities, but they must first make the residents aware of these resources.

LIBRARY AS ACCESS TO DIGITAL RESOURCES, DIGITAL CONTENT, AND TECHNOLOGIES

Whether there are books or bytes in a library, what matters most are the user communities the library serves. From the perspective of the library collection, there are still similarities to be found between various libraries, mainly when analyzing the physical collections and digital content. Marchionini and Fox (1999) pointed out that digital library work contains a complex design space shaped by four dimensions: community, technology, services, and content. They commented:

> Because information is a basic human need and libraries have evolved into an important institution to help communities of humans communicate in spite of differences in time and space, one key dimension of the design space is labeled "community" and reflects social, economic, political, legal and cultural issues. This dimension includes the needs, information-seeking behaviors and attitudes of the individuals within a community. This dimension is exceedingly complex and has to date received the least amount of attention. (p. 219)

The context of the quotation above is around the concept of digital libraries, but the quotation also reflects how libraries help users access both print and digital resources, creating digital content in social media, and utilizing digital resources. Rural library directors and staff members should keep in mind that digital or print collections are for the community that the library serves and are to meet the needs of community users' social, economic, political, legal, and cultural issues.

QUALITIES NEEDED IN A LIBRARY DIRECTOR AND ANY STAFF

To help users of varying intellectual and technological abilities make good use of the diverse formats found in library collections, librarians need to utilize a number of different library management skills. Financial and personnel skills are probably the two most important management skills needed for small libraries. The library manager must be able choose which databases to purchase and how to use them once they are in the collection, and this is part of the financial planning and fiscal management process. It is common to see rural and small libraries managed by one staff member, and there is often a need to hire or lead the part-time staff members or volunteers in rural library projects.

In addition to information organization and searching skills, they must also teach users how to access the digital and online resources, but not all librarians have anticipated becoming instructors. Instruction is also part of communication skill set that will be essential in order to promote the library's services to the governing board and advisors. Jordan (2003) suggested that first-year library managers work closely with boards, conducting community involvement projects, seeking grants, and training the staff, all of which requires librarians to have good personal skills in order to excel in the communities.

COMMUNITY FACTORS

The concept of community has different meanings, so "community" needs to be defined before one seeks local community support for the library. These meanings will be provided here.

Definition of Community

A rural sociologist defined community as "a number of families residing in a relatively small area within which they have developed a more or less complete sociocultural system imbued with collective identification and by means of which they solve problems arising from the sharing of the area" (Sutton & Kolaja, 1960; also cited by Wilkinson, 1991). Flora and Flora (2012) emphasized the term "community" as a place or location in which people interact for mutual benefits. Each community has its own unique values and community assets that can be analyzed via its cultural, human, social, political, and financial capitals; the community itself is diverse but may not necessarily offer its members all the services that individuals require (p. 29).

Another definition of community is proposed by MacQueen:

A common definition of community emerged as a group of people with diverse characteristics who are linked by social ties, share common perspectives, and engage in joint action in geographical locations or settings. The participants differed in the emphasis they placed on particular elements of the definition. Community was defined similarly but experienced differently by people with diverse backgrounds. (MacQueen et al., 2001, p. 1929)

Another definition found in human management literature emphasizes the community as a factor in an individual's life. Bookman (2005) defined a community as the "geographical area that serves as the context for both work life and family life," (p. 1929). A community also includes the physical environment, infrastructure (such as mass transit), demographic profiles, social support, and academic resources such as libraries and schools (Ng & Feldman, 2013). All of these definitions help us understand a generic community; however, there are urban and rural communities, and they may be defined differently. This book focuses on the rural community.

Rural Communities

Rural is defined depending on the context. Governments often label rural areas based on the size of the population, possibly for administrative purposes. The U.S. Census defined rural as a township with a population of less than 2,500 (http://www.census.gov/population/censusdata/urdef.txt). Another definition of rural is nonmetropolitan counties. According to this definition, nearly two-thirds of the nation's 3,142 counties are rural, and these rural communities comprise 17% of the population, including 49 million people, and about 80% of the country's total land area (United States Department of Agriculture Economic Research Service, n.d.). However, both definitions have their limitations of not describing the interaction between rural communities and surrounding geographical entities.

Flora and Flora (2012) reminded us that rural communities are diverse both geographically and geologically, ranging from mountains, mines, farms, retirement communities, and Native American reservations to bedroom communities and so forth. Such diversity makes rural communities differ from each other on environmental, social, and economic challenges. Economically, rural areas are often used for the production and extraction of natural resources, such as farms, prairies, forests, and ranches. The report *Supporting Sustainable Rural Communities*, by the U.S. Department of Transportation, the U.S. Department of Housing and Urban Development, and the U.S. Environmental Protection Agency (2011), described the challenges of rural communities:

> Resource-based economies are vulnerable to the impacts of commodity prices, technological changes, land value dynamics, and other market influences. Some communities whose economies are contracting are experiencing unemployment, poverty, population loss, the aging of their workforces, and increasing demands for social services with fewer dollars to pay for them. In some rural areas, these are not new trends, but generations-old issues. Additionally, residents of remote communities have limited access to jobs, services, and transportation options. Long, expensive commutes to distant employment centers can eat up a large percentage of the family budget, or families have to live sparsely on the small amount of local work available. People who don't have access to personal vehicles or who do not drive, such as low income residents and senior citizens, lack mobility and have even less access to jobs, healthcare, and other services. (p. 3)

Small sizes and isolation may contribute to the reasons why rural communities are considered to be a relatively disadvantaged social ecosystem compared with their urban and suburban counterparts. These areas usually have a low density of population; limited investments in transportation, housing development, and economic development; and limited government investment in facilities.

Information technologies, globalizations, economic development, and a shift of lifestyles may link the rural communities closer to their urban and suburban counterparts, and recently government funding has become available for the development of rural communities. For example, the importance of rural development brought together three government agencies: the U.S. Department of Transportation, the U.S. Department of Housing and Urban Development, and the U.S. Environmental Protection Agency, together forming an interagency Partnership for Sustainable Communities (United States Environmental Protection Agency, 2011). This partnership allows rural communities to apply funds to invest in rural town centers, housing development, affordable housing, transportation access, and so forth.

Community Support

Community support can be reflected by a library's level of public engagement, which is defined in a Pew Research report as the perception of the importance of public libraries in the residents' lives, the usage of libraries, and the view on the role of libraries in communities (Zickuhr, Purcell, & Rainie, 2014). Pew Research suggested that those high engagement groups are those who "value and utilize public libraries most heavily—those who say that libraries play a major role in their own lives and in the lives of their families, who think libraries improve their communities, who are avid readers and think libraries play an essential role in encouraging literacy and a love of reading," and there are also those low engagement groups who seldom use libraries, museum, or bookstores (http://www.pewinternet.org/2014/03/13/summary-of-findings-4/#_About_this_Typology).

The engagement in public libraries was analyzed in the Pew Research Report as cited above that surveyed 6,224 Americans ages 16 and older. The survey reported that public engagement with public libraries differs in urban, suburban, and rural communities. They found that residents who have high engagement with public libraries accounted for 20% of those surveyed, residents with medium engagement accounted for 48%, residents with low engagement accounted for 16%, and residents with no personal library accounted for 18%. At the same time, while high engagement was greater in urban (35%) and suburban (31%) communities, medium engagement in urban (34%) and suburban (40%) were both lower; and the number of low engagement and no engagement residents in urban and suburban communities remained similar. Lower community engagement hints at less support for a library.

A lower amount of high engagement in rural libraries puts rural libraries in a disadvantaged position when directly competing with other city units on budgetary and financial resource allocations. There seems to be more room in rural communities to convert medium engaging library users to strong supporters using a variety of methods. With limited resources available in rural communities, it is even more important for libraries to partner with other community groups, and sometimes partnership is the only way to achieve community support due to internal competition in a community. The amount of the community support is a good indicator of how successful a library is, as community support implies that a library's services meet the needs of the constituents it serves. Understanding community factors is the foundation needed in order to serve culturally diverse community users.

Various restrictions and barriers to the use of library services may occur in a community in terms of social, cultural, and technological restrictions on accessing information, but these can be minimized if the library staff understands the community users. Demographics of a community may impact the library's community support. There might be various restrictions and barriers to the use of library services in a community in terms of social, cultural, and technological restrictions on accessing the information. Ruhlmann (2014) found that some Latino immigrants might not access the resources available because they are afraid that a library is a government entity and might give them trouble regarding their immigration status, or they simply fear that a library will abuse their personal information. WebJunction published a research report on Latinos' public library use with 3,058 users, and the researchers recommended that librarians inform their community that the libraries do not share library user information (Flores & Pachon, 2008). They found that foreign-born Latinos are much less likely to use the library for fear of signing up for a library card and hence losing personal confidential information. The same study also found that only 47% of Latinos who use the library have Internet access at home or work, which is considerably lower than the national average. Such an understanding of the communities in their own area can greatly help librarians when reaching out to multiple user groups and when building relevant library programs.

A librarian needs to understand the library's users and community needs in order to build collections according to user needs. Strategies are available to instruct librarians on how to gain the maximum support for such libraries, and we will discuss these concepts and strategies in coming chapters.

CONCLUSION

Understanding a small library's funding sources, its diverse users, its collections, and the library's place as an educational opportunity is the beginning of the process of managing a small or rural library. It is common that public libraries are funded by local venues, including local city and country tax revenues, private donations, grants, and other income. Oftentimes librarians report directly to those who should be stakeholders in their communities, such as city managers, mayors, or county judges; it is very important to allow stakeholders and communities supporting the library to be aware of the evidence of library successes in building diverse collections and serving diverse users among their constituents.

Providing access to digital resources and the qualities needed for a director are equally important. Finally, defining the community is another first step in strengthening the role of the library in the society so it will have a greater impact on the daily lives of its citizens. Among library collections, users, and communities, serving user needs is the main purpose of building diverse collections and the engagement of communities. Libraries as a space should connect users and information sources, save users' time, and become an essential community asset. It is important for library directors to serve diverse users in their communities and maximize various tangible and intangible support. Raising funds to support the library is becoming a joint effort by both the library and its communities, once library service is focused on its community and its users' needs. At the same time librarians today must respond to challenges and enhance community engagement. Understanding community factors will likely lead to community support and enhance the success of library services. The following chapters will discuss in detail concepts and methods that contribute to successful user services in digital age.

REFERENCES

American Library Association. (2014). *Library operating expenditures: A selected annotated bibliography.* Chicago, IL: American Library Association. Available at http://www.ala.org/tools/libfactsheets/alalibraryfactsheet04

Augst, T., & Wiegand, W. (2003). *Libraries as agencies of culture.* Madison, WI: The University of Wisconsin Press.

Benton Foundation. (1997). Buildings, books, and bytes: Libraries and communities in the digital age. *Library Trends, 46*(1), 78–223.

Bobinski, G. S. (1969). *Carnegie libraries: Their history and impact on American public library development.* Chicago, IL: American Library Association.

Bookman, A. (2005). Can employers be good neighbors? Redesigning the workplace-community interface. In S. M. Bianchi, L. M. Casper, & R. B. King (Eds.), *Work, family, health, and well-being* (pp. 141–156). Mahwah, NJ: Erlbaum.

Boyce, J. I., & Boyce, B. R. (1995). Library outreach programs in rural areas. *Library Trends, 44*(1), 112–128.

Case, D. (2012). *Looking for information: A survey of research on information seeking, needs, and behavior.* Bingley, United Kingdom: Emerald Group.

Chant, I. (2014). Gates Foundation prepares to exit library ecosystem. *Library Journal, 139*(11), 12. Available at http://lj.libraryjournal.com/2014/05/budgets-funding/gates-foundation-prepares-to-exit-library-ecosystem/#_

Davis, D. G., Jr., & Tucker, J. M. (1989). *American library history: A comprehensive guide to the literature.* Santa Barbara, CA: ABC-CLIO.

Dayal, B. (2011). *Managing academic libraries: Principles and practice*. New Delhi, India: Isha Books.

Dervin, B. (1992). From the mind's eye of the user: The sense-making qualitative-quantitative methodology. In J. Glazier & R. R. Powell (Eds.), *Qualitative research in information management* (pp. 61–84). Santa Barbara, CA: Libraries Unlimited.

Edwards, J. B., Rauseo, M. S., & Unger, K. R. (2013). Community centered: 23 reasons why your library is the most important place in town. *Public Libraries Online* (April 30, 2013). Available at http://publiclibrariesonline.org/2013/04/community-centered-23-reasons-why-your-library-is-the-most-important-place-in-town/

Evans, G. E., & Zarnosky, M. R. (2000). *Developing library and information center collections* (4th ed.). Englewood, CO: Libraries Unlimited.

Flora, C. B., & Flora, J. L. (2012). *Rural communities: Legacy and change* (4th ed.). Boulder, CO: Westview Press.

Flores, E., & Pachon, H. (2008). *Latinos and public library perceptions*. Los Angeles, CA: Tomás Rivera Policy Institute. Available at http://www.webjunction.org/content/dam/WebJunction/Documents/webJunction/213544usb_wj_latinos_and_public_library_perceptions.pdf

Institute of Museum and Library Services. (2013). *Total collection expenditures of public libraries and percentage distribution of expenditures, by type of expenditure and state: Fiscal year 2011*. Washington, DC: Institute of Museum and Library Services. Available at http://www.imls.gov/assets/1/AssetManager/FY2011_PLS_Tables_20-30A.pdf

Johnson, P. (2009). *Fundamentals of collection development and management*. Chicago, IL: American Library Association.

Jordan, M. W. (2003). Surviving your first year as library director. *Public Libraries, 42*(July/August), 215–217.

Kelley, M. (2012). The new normal: Annual library budgets survey 2012. *Library Journal, 137*(1), 37–40. Available at http://lj.libraryjournal.com/2012/01/funding/the-new-normal-annual-library-budgets-survey-2012/#_

Kelly, T. (1966). *Early public libraries: A history of public libraries in Great Britain before 1850*. London, United Kingdom: The Library Association.

Krotoski, A. (2011). Youth culture: Teenage kicks in the digital age. *The Guardian* (June 25, 2011). Available at http://www.theguardian.com/technology/2011/jun/26/untangling-web-krotoski-youth-culture

MacQueen, K. M., McLellan, E., Metzger, D. S., Kegeles, S., Strauss, R. P., & Scotti, R., et al. (2001). What is community? An evidence-based definition for participatory public health. *American Journal of Public Health, 91*(12), 1929–1938. Available at http://www.ncbi.nlm.nih.gov/pmc/articles/PMC1446907/

Marchionini, G., & Fox, E. A. (1999). Progress toward digital libraries: Augmentation through integration. *Information Processing & Management, 35*(3), 219–225.

Maslow, A. H. (1968). *Toward a psychology of being*. New York: D. Van Nostrand.

McMullen, H. (2000). *American libraries before 1876*. Westport, CT: Greenwood.

Mehra, B., & Braquet, D. (2007). Library and information science professionals as community action researchers in an academic setting: Top ten directions to further institutional change for people of diverse sexual orientations and gender identities. *Library Trends, 56*(2), 542–565.

Naidoo, J. C. (2014). *The importance of diversity in library programs and material collections for children*. Association for Library Services to Children. Chicago,

IL: American Library Association. Available at http://www.ala.org/alsc/sites/ala
.org.alsc/files/content/ALSCwhitepaper_importance%20of%20diversity_with%20
graphics_FINAL.pdf

Ng, T. W., & Feldman, D. C. (2013). Community embeddedness and work outcomes: The
mediating role of organizational embeddedness. *Human Relations, 67*(1), 71–103.

Peterson, L. (1999). The definition of diversity: Two views, a more specific definition.
In M. Winston (Ed.), *Managing multiculturalism and diversity in the library: Principles and issues for administrators* (pp. 17–26). Philadelphia, PA: Haworth Press.

Ranganathan, S. R., & Gopinath, M. A. (1966). *Library book selection.* Bombay, India:
Asia Publishing House.

Richards, P. S., Wiegand, W. A., & Dalbello, M. (2015). *A history of modern librarianship:
Constructing the heritage of western cultures.* Santa Barbara, CA: Libraries Unlimited.

Riva, C. (2001). *The Bill & Melinda Gates Foundation's U.S. Library Program
distributes final round of grant application.* Seattle, WA: The Bill and Melinda
Gates Foundation. Available at http://www.gatesfoundation.org/Media-Center/Press
-Releases/2001/02/US-Library-Program-Grants

Ruhlmann, E. (2014). Connecting Latinos with libraries. *American Libraries, 45*(5),
36–40. Available at http://americanlibrariesmagazine.org/2014/05/19/connecting
-latinos-with-libraries/

Shoham, S., & Strauss, S. K. (2008). Immigrants' information needs: Their role in
the absorption process. *Information Research, 13*(4). Available at http://www
.informationr.net/ir/13-4/paper359.html

Sutton, W. A., Jr., & Kolaja, J. (1960). The concept of community. *Rural Sociology,
25*(2), 197–203.

Todaro, J. (2012). *Public library advisory board handbook, 2012.* Austin, TX: Texas
State Library and Archives Commission. Available at https://www.tsl.state.tx.us/ld
/pubs/plant/index.html

Totten, H., Garner, C., & Brown, R. W. (1996). *Culturally diverse library collections
for youth.* New York: Neal Schuman.

United States Census. (2008). Population: Religion [Data file]. Available at http://www
.census.gov/compendia/statab/cats/population/religion.html

United States Census. (2010). How do we know? America's foreign born in the last
50 years [Data file]. Available at http://www.census.gov/library/infographics/foreign
_born.html

United States Census. (2013). U.S. census state and country quick facts [Data file].
Available at http://quickfacts.census.gov/qfd/states/00000.html

United States Department of Agriculture Economic Research Service. (n.d.). *Rural
population and migration briefing room.* Washington, DC: United States Department of Agriculture. Available at http://www.ers.usda.gov/Briefing/Population/

United States Environmental Protection Agency. (2011). *Supporting Sustainable Rural
Communities* (Report number EPA 231-K-11-001). Washington, DC: United States
Environmental Protection Agency. Available at: http://www.epa.gov/sites/production
/files/documents/2011_11_supporting-sustainable-rural-communities.pdf

Wilkinson, K. P. (1991). The community in rural America (No. 95). Santa Barbara, CA:
Greenwood Publishing Group.

Zickuhr, K., Purcell, K., & Rainie, L. (2014). *Distance admirers to library loves—and
beyond: Summary of findings.* Washington, DC: Pew Research Center. Retrieved
from http://www.pewinternet.org/2014/03/13/summary-of-findings-4/

CHAPTER TWO

Improving Community Outreach

To make better use of community resources, managers of small libraries must become masters of conducting community outreach and partnership projects. They do this to maintain a successful presence in their communities. The ability to reach out to communities is one of the most important professional competencies for librarians, especially for small libraries. In other words, managers need to know that one of the most important professional competencies for librarians in library services is the ability to reach out to communities, and this is especially necessary with a small communities. While this is pointed out in the Reference and User Services Association, a division of the American Library Association (ALA), which provides guidelines that emphasize a reference librarian's ability to effectively communicate to users and promote services to users (Reference and User Services Association, 2003), it is equally true for all services. Library outreach is reflected in multiple ways through the programs offered in the library, including collaborative programs and joint events with community members and, more formally, partnerships with community members that will share the cost or revenues on joint efforts.

This chapter discusses the history of library outreach services and venues of community outreach and partnership. All these efforts are for the purpose of building a community-centered library. The chapter closes with suggestions for creating community outreach plans and shares examples of some successful outreach plans from rural and small libraries.

HISTORY OF OUTREACH SERVICES

We will start with the definition of outreach and then review the early history of outreach. We will then discuss bookmobiles that are still used today.

Definition of Outreach

The *Online Dictionary for Library and Information Science* (Reitz, 2014) defines outreach as "Library programs and services designed to meet the information needs of users who are unserved or underserved, for example, those who are visually impaired, homebound, institutionalized, not fluent in the national language, illiterate, or marginalized in some other way" (http://www.abc-clio.com/ODLIS/odlis_o.aspx). Outreach has particular function in the expansion of library services to larger potential user groups.

For this book, the definition of outreach includes the effort to create *awareness* about library services and to promote the *value* of library work. Library outreach activities bring in potential users who otherwise may not approach libraries and utilize library resources and services.

Historically library outreach started with individuals or organizations reaching out to special groups, for example, as a provider of books for the African American community, for ships, for traveling libraries, and for tribal libraries and as book mobile services that extended the library's services beyond its geographical limitation to remote areas. In recent years, the concept of outreach has expanded to encompass the philosophy of social inclusion and social well-being, as well as a recent new focus on serving linguistic minorities.

Early Library Outreach

Freeman and Hvode (2003) compiled a collection of essays on the topic of the early history of library outreach. These essays were based on programs from the ALA's Library History Round Table in 1999. These historical reviews provided snapshots of outreach programs in the 19th and 20th centuries in the United States. One essay described the existence of social libraries that included a collection of books gathered and owned cooperatively for the communal use of persons who organized themselves for that purpose, in the New Orleans area in the early 1800s. Another discussed the life of Miss Essae Martha Culver, a white woman, who brought books to the African American residents of Louisiana's bayou area, during the time of segregation and prejudice (Jumonville, 2003, p. 22). In one parish, the Webster Parish, African Americans composed half of the population of 24,700 but were scattered over five hundred square miles. The parish library served as a model for cooperation and outreach in the early 19th century.

The concept of libraries spread to the whole country, from land to seas. For example, Hovde (2003) described the Little Red Box, a mobile library with books loaned to ships for sailors to read, which could then be transferred to another ship for a new set of books (p. 54). It was administered by the American Seamen's Friend Society from 1859 to the 1940s.

An example of traveling libraries is the one developed by the American librarian and educator Melvil Dewey, the founder of Dewey Decimal Classification. He established a traveling library when he served as the director of the New York State Library (Watson, 2003).

The ALA formed the Committee on Work with the Foreign Born (ALA CWFB) in 1918 and began promoting reading to immigrants and teaching them the English language in order to prepare for their naturalization, particularly those foreign-born who might not have the opportunity of formal language training (Jones, 2003). In addition, outreach services by public libraries were expanded to building libraries in American Indian tribes, largely sponsored by federal programs. Today both the federal government and many states provide funding supporting the expansion of libraries in tribal libraries (Patterson, 2003).

Bookmobiles in Rural Areas

Bookmobiles expanded the library service area and provided access to remote residents. The first U.S. bookmobile was started in 1905 by Mary Titcomb, who was the librarian of the Washington County Free Library in Maryland (http://www.ala.org/offices/olos/nbdhome). Inspired by the British small mobile libraries in the century, Titcomb developed a horse-drawn library wagon to send books to nearby general stores and post offices in rural communities. Within a short period of time, there were 66 deposit stations throughout the county, and history witnessed the first motorized bookmobiles in 1912 (http://www.pbs.org/pov/biblioburro/bookmobile.php). The number of bookmobiles in the United States fluctuates. For example, there were 921 in use in 1989 and 879 in 2001 (http://www.ala.org/research/librarystats/public/bookmobiles/bookmobilesu). Many libraries still use bookmobiles to extend their services such as e-books, e-readers, iPads, and computer stations to remote populations, schools, and senior citizens (Warburton, 2013). For example, in 2012, Mineola Memorial Library in Mineola, Texas, implemented a bookmobile program as their outreach project (Moore, 2012).

In 2015, the ALA Office for Diversity and other national small library organizations coordinated the first National Bookmobile Day on April 15. Many libraries and private donors are still willing to fund bookmobiles since they extend library services to socially excluded groups who live in remote areas and to senior citizens in retirement homes who are physically unable to drive to libraries.

Every library serves a community with unique geographic, demographic, and statistical characteristics. A library plays an important role in its community partnership and outreach activities in order to improve the public's perception of the value of the library.

VENUES OF COMMUNITY OUTREACH
AND PERCEPTIONS OF VALUE

Partially due to the evolving technologies incorporated in people's lives, many public libraries face the challenges as the public diminishes the value of public libraries' services, which in turn has reduced funding support. Libraries in small cities or communities are particularly affected by declining tax bases and funding allocations. Libraries need to have stakeholders, preferably city managers, as their advocates to ensure stable funding support.

The foundation of the success of libraries lies in the belief that libraries are a public value. When a library is underappreciated as a community asset, it is in a disadvantageous position when competing for community resources. It is often because the library is not viewed as an essential element in community life (Blake, Martin, & Du, 2011). A library in such situation needs to strengthen the concept that it is an essential element of community life, as a community-centered entity that creates tremendous social values.

Library outreach services can come in many formats. These include serving remote populations, sponsoring programs for minorities and other underserved populations, and reaching out to users who otherwise will not be able to use the library and appreciate library services.

> Herb Landau, at the time, the director from Milanof-Schock Library from Mount Joy, Pennsylvania, purchased a used van and turned it into the "Reads on Wheels" outreach program, which delivered books and audio-visual materials to homebound individuals. One 98-year-old homebound retiree borrowed a computer and received tutorship from the library. She also borrowed a video player and watched a movie that she hadn't see in 15 years. The library serves 20,000 residents in a 50 square mile district, and the library has become the core of the community. The library was also named the Best Small Library of the Year in 2006 (Berry, 2006).

This is an example of a library serving remote populations. In today's digital world, unserved populations not only include geographically remote areas but also include people in rural, suburban, and urban areas who are marginalized by digital information technologies.

Librarians from Honey Grove, Texas, a small town about 90 miles northeast of Dallas, Texas, observed a special group of library visitors belonging to the Mennonite Church. The Mennonites, a conservative Christian denomination, emigrated in the 18th century from Europe, as they were fleeing the religious persecution (Kraybill, Bowman, & Bowman, 2001, p. 5). Many of the Mennonites still maintain traditional practices. Because members of the younger generation could not find jobs outside of farming, a few of them visited the Honey Grove Library to seek help on obtaining their General Educational Development (GED) diplomas. The library sponsored GED classes for this particular group, and eventually the class grew to more than 30 people. The library was named one of the finalists of *Library Journal*'s Best Small Libraries in America award in 2014 for its excellent service.

Today, public libraries are one of the most ubiquitous of all American institutions, more widespread than Starbucks or McDonald's (Morris, 2011). A survey from the Institute of Museums and Library Services (IMLS) (2011) indicated that all categories of public library use have increased, including visitation, circulation, program attendance, use of public-access Internet computers, and reference transactions. Rudin (2008) predicted that even for most people, the library in its most basic function as a source of information is becoming a virtual destination, and people still want to come to a library if it is updated and well equipped and if it has an inviting environment. This will particularly need to be the perception of the library if partnership and collaboration are a norm in the community.

PARTNERSHIP AND COLLABORATION

An effective way to demonstrate a public value and impact is to develop a coalition or partnership around a particular issue or specific problem in the community, reaching out to certain user groups or other organizations that also feel passionately about similar issues.

Health Information Services

Librarians may provide training on the access of health information to its community members, collaborate with local businesses, and sponsor various community health affairs to promote the well-being of its community users. Health information access and use is personal yet challenging and requires information-evaluation-skills training that a library traditionally provides to the communities' residents. Many public health challenges such as health disparities are complex and multifactorial, requiring a sustained commitment, a broad vision, and a willingness to collaborate (Cogdill, 2007).

One example of community collaboration can be related to public health information seeking. Although the Internet enables many users to seek health-related information online, many community residents are interested in community health fairs where various services are performed by health professionals. For example, the Motley County Library, in Matador, Texas, located approximately 80 miles northeast of Lubbock, Texas, partnered with The Motley County Clinic, the primary health care facility for Matador and the surrounding area and hosted a community health fair in 2012. According to the 2010 Census, the population of Motley County is 1,210. The event developed programs that increased patron participation and increased patron familiarity with electronic and digital resources (Meador, 2012).

Public libraries may gain community interest and support when they collaborate with health organizations by providing health information services via outreach. There are various benefits of public health information outreach, and collaboration and partnership can emerge as a result of such projects. For short-term projects and activities, collaborations between libraries and other organizations can "provide access to resources and expertise that might not otherwise be available. Longer-term outreach partnerships have the potential for transforming libraries" (Cogdill, 2007, p. 290).

Reaching Out to Potential Users

Sometimes librarians cannot reach out to a certain potential user group due to various limitations, and they may find it more efficient to partner with agencies that already have connections with such populations. Diaz (2005) outlined plans for libraries to serve migrant farm workers; migrant farm workers rarely use the library because they have concerns about privacy, library fees, schedules of time to visit the library, transportation, immigration status, English literacy level, and self-esteem, among others. Libraries can collaborate with other agencies to offer information services to migrant workers, such as the following:

> organizations that deal directly with farm workers: schools and adult education centers; federally funded migrant Head Start programs and other child-care programs; after-school programs; health clinics; prenatal facilities; public health outreach programs; public assistance agencies; community policing law enforcement programs; correctional facilities; legal-aid programs; public parks and recreation centers; churches; nonprofit charities; community service volunteer organizations; labor organizations and even foreign consulates and embassies. (p. 12)

One of the challenges when providing services to immigrants is the variation of literacy skills. Many may be able to read in their native language, while others may have had very little education. Enhancing the community literacy level can potentially improve education, employment, health, and social outcome. For example, Kong (2013) reported the success of the California Library Literacy Services, an agency that funds adult basic education tutoring for all programs. The majority of the cost of this program is paid by the local or county libraries, so that the libraries can provide "free early literacy to young people, conversation classes to immigrants, computer skills to job seekers," and other technology classes to the community (Kong, 2013, p. 41). Funded by their Friends of the Library, in the King County Library System, Washington, librarians formulated two book discussion groups in other languages—one in Chinese and one in Spanish—and brought community users together by providing a platform for non-English immigrants to appreciate their own cultures (Pender & Garcia, 2013).

Similar collaborative efforts have been made by libraries internationally. In Victoria, Australia, the Casey-Cardinia Library Corporation and Windermere Child and Family Services have cosponsored a partnership program, Library Has Legs, in order to help children ages 0–5 with early literacy programs (Smith, 2008). All partnership efforts demonstrate the benefits of library literacy programs in their communities.

Partnership is not limited to organizations in a community: families can be partners, too. To promote family literacy, Hill and Diamond (2013) promoted shared book reading programs to promote early literacy, including the Lap-Sit family literacy for babies and toddlers, and the Dads' program family literacy session for preschoolers, and the Parents as Partners programs for school-aged children. Such programs can be a great tool to promote libraries in diverse communities where family culture is more emphasized. In return, strong collaborative partners increase the chance of success for both sides.

Gashurov and Kendrick (2013) reviewed the principles of how to make partnerships work and found that it is important for partners to approach the issue strategically, with an end goal and a culture of collaborative and commitments in mind. They concluded that collaborators with deep commitments may achieve greater impacts (http://lj.libraryjournal.com/2013/10/managing-libraries/collaboration-for-hard-times/#_). They believe that collaboration is a critical aspect of organizational life, while identifying the right partner for a supportive relationship is not an easy task. The process involves risks and costs, and "the tension between self-interest and resource sharing" (Gashurov & Kendrick, 2013). Library practitioners may find potential mutually beneficial partners using digital technologies and solidify collaboration by sharing the same missions and goals among partners.

The digital environment brings opportunities for libraries to partner with local organizations and peer libraries. For example, the Library at Cedar Creek Lake in Texas has partnered with the Texas Workforce Commission for outreach events, including a job fair that was held in the library and a Texas Workforce Commission mobile unit helping unemployed people fill out job applications. The library also promoted the services of the library's databases and resources for job seekers. Small public libraries that are dependent on city or county tax support particularly need to seek partners to expand their services. Small libraries can advance community integration by working with other units, such as the fire station, the police, and other law-enforcement units. Such partnership may send a signal to the communities that the libraries are not just competing for the resources or the very existence of themselves but instead enhancing the community value as a whole. For example, Alpine Public Libraries partnered with the Border Patrol Wives group and sponsored a youth reading program for a humorous competitive gaming event (Delaney, 2012).

Libraries often do not have enough resources for all of the needed projects, but with partnerships, libraries can use these potential partners to maximize community resources. The collaborative process needs to be mutually beneficial, so all parties can sustain and grow. In the previous section on the partnership stories of the Honey Grove Library and the Fannin County Literacy Association were both successful.

The above examples demonstrate the principle of successful partnership and collaboration. Strong advocacy programs require library leaders to demonstrate the impact of activities and services. Moreover, collaborative efforts serve as advocacy catalysts that demonstrate the worth of libraries to stakeholders including community leaders, friends of libraries, elected officials, and resource allocators. Once a library broadens the support around an issue of common interest, it can usually achieve success. Collaborating with community partners to implement programs and events can promote the social value of both units, and at the same time, libraries can become more community-centered partners during the collaboration process.

COMMUNITY-CENTERED LIBRARY

The concept of a community-centered library was addressed in the book *Transforming Libraries, Building Communities: The Community-Centered Library* (Edwards, Robinson, & Unger, 2013) as a new model that goes beyond information access and focuses on how people in the communities use the information, services, and programming that a library provides (p. 3). Edwards, Rauseo, and Unger (2013) also suggested that libraries bring values to communities in the following areas: as community builders, as community centers for diverse populations, as centers for the arts, as universities, and as champions of youth. These are the guidelines for librarians to use to establish the library's role as a community-centered library.

Blake, Martin, and Du (2011) emphasized that rural libraries should proceed from the point of view of the library but also take into consideration the community's needs, wants, and priorities. Characteristics of a community-centered library include the following:

1. The library's priority is on providing services to the individuals, organizations, businesses, and institutions in the community.
2. The library recognizes it exists because of the community and for the community.
3. The library staff knows people, not things, come first.
4. The library actively solicits input from various segments of the community.
5. The library facilitates partnerships between it and other agencies or between citizens groups and appropriate organizations.
6. Partnerships are beneficial to both the library and the partner (p. 52).

Library services such as children and youth programming, reference services, and outreach programs may increase residents' sense of community and thus help to retain local talent and increase the business and cultural values in a small community. A library may also strengthen its value in a community by establishing partnerships, strong advocacy programs, and other service areas.

The following is a successful case of when a library designed a center for literacy and arts:

> The library will offer a series of music development workshops. These will be held every three months with the first being in December. It will be called "It's Music, Music, Music at the Quitman Public Library!" Mark Shelton, bandleader

of the group Tin Roof Tango, will lead the multi-cultural workshop and program that includes an array of acoustical folk instruments and world music repertoire. The workshop is scheduled to maximize attendance and interest by wrapping up an eventful two days following the "Friday Night Acoustical Jam Fever at the Quitman Public Library" and "Music on the Streets in Downtown Mineola." It will be open to any age person or skill level. (Allen, 2012, p. 7)

With community-centeredness in mind, libraries can build successful community outreach plans and make an impact on the rural and small communities. The next section will discuss how to create a meaningful outreach plan.

CREATING A COMMUNITY OUTREACH PLAN

Successful community outreach projects need well-designed outreach plans. The community outreach plan can be informal and formal. The informal plans can include a simple statement of the purpose of the plan, a general description of the program and who will be served, and a description of how the plan will be implemented. A formal outreach plan is a more in-depth, professional research process.

The formal outreach plan provides the structure of outreach activities while keeping project flexibility. To design a community outreach plan, a library director needs to understand the community needs and have an estimate of the community assets. Needs assessment is a systematic process for collecting and analyzing information using one or more data-collection techniques (Blake, Martin, & Du, 2011). Such techniques include surveys, focus group interviews, observations, and other qualitative or quantitative methods, and they provide a systematic inventory of a full picture of positive aspects of the community and the library. Chapter 10 discusses in detail the collection data on communities, user needs assessment, and various techniques.

Another important aspect in community outreach planning is to align the community outreach plans with a library's mission, goals, and objectives. Missions, goals, and objectives are usually part of an organization's strategic plan, and they are the guidelines of a library's resource allocation in the short-, medium-, and long-terms operations.

Since the community outreach plan is the result of multiple stages of joint efforts between the library, users, and community partners, in case there is a change in a library's leadership, a well-designed community outreach plan provides a document for the library to continue the common efforts and reduces the need to start the plan from scratch.

The University of North Texas PEARL project (Promoting & Enhancing the Advancement of Rural Libraries) was funded by the Robert and Ruby Priddy Charitable Trust, the Priddy Foundation, and the University of North Texas to advance the role of rural libraries in local communities through collaborative programs and educational opportunities. The participating libraries completed 104 community outreach plans that are listed on the project website (http://pearl.unt.edu). These plans were composed by libraries participating in this project from 2010–2014. Libraries developed various outreach programs according to their local strategic plans and community user needs. The development of outreach plans starts with a community asset analysis, user survey and needs analysis, community partner identification, outreach plan design and implementation, and evaluation. For details of developing a community plan, please refer to the handbook by Blake, Martin, and Du (2011). The benefit of having these community outreach plans available is to allow libraries in various sizes to borrow ideas of community outreach and partner with other organizations. Many of these models can be replicated. Libraries that participated in the project have often reused the community data collected for outreach projects for new grant proposals and have had a higher success rate than previously.

The following is an example of one outreach plan:

> Waurika Public Library will conduct a series of monthly book discussions during the 12:00 noon–1:00 p.m. lunch hour. This is intended to be a pilot project. If there is interest in continuing it, the library will make it an ongoing program. They will be held the second Thursday of each month. The pilot program dates are October 10, November 14, and December 12, in 2013, and January 9 and February 13, 2014. Waurika Public Library Community Outreach Plan Two lunch discussions will take place at the library, two at local restaurants, and one at the Senior Citizen Center. The library director will review two book titles to open the discussions and give brief information about the book author. Program attendees will each have an opportunity to share what they are reading, swap books, socialize with other readers in the community, and make book recommendations to other program attendees. The lunch programs will be called, "Booked for Lunch" and are intended to be for adults. The library intends to partner with Friends of Waurika Public Library, the Senior Citizen Center, Bills Fish House and Nikki's Café. The book discussions are meant to be casual and to encourage meaningful conversation between adults, while also introducing books that the library offers. (Watkins, 2013, p. 6)

Library outreach programs can address many of the common issues in a community: health information access, computer skills, youth gaming programs, English language programs, Spanish conversation classes, books on movies, summer reading programs, book clubs, family literacy, e-books, and literacy programs to people with special needs, and so on.

CONCLUSIONS

Based on the cases we listed in the chapter, one should conclude that libraries began community outreach in their earliest days and that they initiated and completed community engagement projects, such as travel libraries and bookmobiles. Community outreach demonstrates how librarians conceptualize the new role of libraries in a community-centered library environment, as they are ready to deliver services outside of the library's physical building to populations who otherwise would not be able to receive the service. As Rovito (2012, p. 61) suggested, "many of the things that drew patrons to libraries in the past—such as access to free information, a quiet place to study or read, and a central community hub—continue to draw them into our buildings. What has changed is our ability to get out from behind our desks and into the community and, parallel to this, the expectation that we will do just that." Community outreach is now becoming one of the most useful professional tools for rural libraries to serve everyone, regardless of their social background, in the communities.

REFERENCES

Allen, D. (2012). *Quitman Public Library outreach plan*. Denton, TX: PEARL Project, University of North Texas. Available at https://pearl.unt.edu/sites/default/files /quitmanpubliclibrary.pdf

Berry, J. N., III. (2006). Everyone's hitching post. *Library Journal, 131*(2), p. 38.

Blake, B., Martin, R., M., & Du, Y. (2011). *Successful community outreach: A how-to-do it manual for librarians*. Chicago, IL: ALA Neal-Schuman.

Cogdill, K. W. (2007). Public health information outreach. *Journal of Medical Library Association, 95*(3), 290–292.

Delaney, P. (2012). *Alpine Public Library community outreach plan*. Denton, TX: PEARL Project, University of North Texas. Available at https://pearl.unt.edu/sites /default/files/alpinepubliclibraryoutreachplan.pdf

Diaz, R. (2005). Developing library outreach programs for migrant farm workers. *Florida Libraries, 48*(1), 12–14.

Edwards, J. B., Rauseo, M. S., & Unger, K. R. (2013). Reasons why your library is the most important place in town. *Public Libraries Online*. Available at http:// publiclibrariesonline.org/2013/04/community-centered-23-reasons-why-your-library -is-the-most-important-place-in-town/

Edwards, J. B., Robinson, M. S., & Unger, K. R. (2013). *Transforming libraries, building communities: The community-centered library*. Lanham, MD: Scarecrow Press.

Freeman, R. S., & Hvode, D. V. (2003). *Libraries to the people: Histories of outreach*. Jefferson, NC: McFarland.

Gashurov, I., & Kendrick, C. L. (2013). Collaboration for hard times. *Library Journal, 138*(18). Available at http://lj.libraryjournal.com/2013/10/managing-libraries /collaboration-for-hard-times/#

Hill, S., & Diamond, A. (2013). Family literacy in response to local contexts. *Australian Journal of Language and Literacy, 36*(1), 48–55.

Hovde, D. M. (2003). Benevolence at sea: Shipboard libraries for the American navy and merchant marine. In R. S. Freeman, & D. V. Hvode (Eds.), *Libraries to the people: Histories of outreach* (pp. 50–72). Jefferson, NC: McFarland.

Institute of Museum and Library Services. (2011). *Public libraries in the United States survey: Fiscal year 2011*. Washington, DC: Institute of Museum and Library Services. Available at http://www.imls.gov/assets/1/AssetManager/PLS2011.pdf

Jones, P. A., Jr. (2003). The ALA Committee on Work with the Foreign Born and the movement to Americanize the immigrant. In R. S Freeman & D. V. Hvode

(Eds.), *Libraries to the people: Histories of outreach* (pp. 96–110). Jefferson, NC: McFarland.

Jumonville, F. M. (2003). Books along the Bayous: Reading materials for two centuries of rural Louisianians. In R. S. Freeman & D. V. Hvode (Eds.), *Libraries to the people: Histories of outreach* (pp. 11–25). Jefferson, NC: McFarland.

Kong, L. (2013). Failing to read well. *Public Libraries, 52*(1), 40–44.

Kraybill, D. B., Bowman, C. B., & Bowman, C. F. (2001). *On the backroad to heaven: Old order Hutterites, Mennonites, Amish, and Brethren.* Baltimore, MD: John Hopkins University Press.

Meador, C. (2012). *Motley County Library community outreach plan.* Denton, TX: PEARL Project, University of North Texas. Available at https://pearl.unt.edu/sites /default/files/motleycountylibrary.pdf

Moore, S. (2012). *Mineola Memorial Library community outreach plan.* Denton, TX: PEARL Project, University of North Texas. Available at https://pearl.unt.edu/sites /default/files/mineola_memorial_library_outreach.pdf

Morris, D. (2011). The public library manifesto: Why libraries matter, and how we can save them. *YES! Magazine.* Available at http://www.yesmagazine.org/happiness /the-public-library-manifesto

Patterson, L. (2003). Historical overview of tribal libraries in the lower forty-eight states. In Freeman, R. S. & D. M. Hovde (Eds.), *Libraries to the people: History of outreach* (pp. 157–162). Jefferson, NC: McFarland.

Pender, W., & Garcia, J. M. (2013). With literacy for all. *Public Libraries, 52*(1), 8–10.

Reference and User Services Association. (2003). RUSA guidelines. Available at http:// www.ala.org/rusa/resources/guidelines

Reitz, J. M. (2014). Online dictionary for library and information science. Santa Barbra, CA: Libraries Unlimited. Available at: http://www.abc-clio.com/ODLIS/odlis_o.aspx

Rovito, J. (2012). Crossing the threshold into the private space: The TD Summer Reading Club Outreach to Shelters Project. *Feliciter, 58*(2), 59–61.

Rudin, P. (2008). No fixed address: The evaluation of outreach library services on university campuses. *The Reference Librarian, 49*(1), 55–75.

Smith, S. (2008). The library has legs: An early childhood literacy outreach program in Victoria. *Aplis, 21*(4), 154–156.

Warburton, B. (2013). Delivering the library. *Library Journal.* Available at http:// lj.libraryjournal.com/2013/09/library-services/delivering-the-library/

Watkins, A. (2013). *Waurika Public Library community outreach plan.* Denton, TX: PEARL Project, University of North Texas. Available at https://pearl.unt.edu/sites /default/files/waurikapubliclibrarycommunityoutreachplan.pdf

Watson, P. D. (2003). Valleys without sunsets: Women's clubs and traveling libraries. In R. S. Freeman, & D. V. Hvode (Eds.), *Libraries to the people: Histories of outreach* (pp. 73–95). Jefferson, NC: McFarland.

CHAPTER THREE

Supporting Social Justice and Rights of Access to Information

Information is one of the basic resources in social life. Organizations and individuals need information for growth and development. While the Internet brought convenience to information access, it also brought inequality for people who don't have literacy skills or technical resources. In this chapter we discuss the issues of inequity and the digital divide. We will start with the concept of social justice and library services and move on to social inclusion, the rights of access to information, and intellectual freedom. The chapter closes with the role of libraries in community users' literacy skills, including users in the rural labor force. For those who are inspired to be a library manager, understanding the concepts of social justice and the right of access to information for all will help to break the barriers and better serve various populations in their communities.

SOCIAL JUSTICE AND LIBRARY SERVICES

Libraries have been providing services equally to everybody in the community, but the concept of social justice has not been discussed until recently. This section will briefly review this concept, followed by the implications in libraries today.

Concept of Social Justice

One of the first to address the term "social justice" was Leo Shields. In his 1941 thesis, "The History and Meaning of the Term Social Justice," he pointed out that the early meaning of social justice was related to a religious social movement. He mentioned the Greek philosopher Aristotle because of the Greek preoccupation with the political virtues, and Aristotle has addressed quite thoroughly the virtue of justice. Shields believed that the more important part on the concept of social justice is the term "justice." Social justice is defined by Shields as "the virtue which governs the relations of members with a society, as such, and the relations of society with its members," which leads to social and individual actions to the general good of the collective body and its members (p. 39).

Recently, Rioux (2010) reviewed the concept of social justice and found that its main concern is how people are treated fairly and have a fair share in that society's benefits. Social justice is becoming a "universally held value" in library services that promotes cultural diversity, human dignity, freedom, and inclusion (p. 14). He suggested that "Western scholars have debated the notion of social justice in many different disciplines, including law, politics, and philosophy" (p. 11). Based on literature, it seems social justice can be one of a core concepts that are related to rural library theory and practice.

Social scientists John Rawls (2001) from Harvard University and David Miller (2001) from Oxford University built rigorous theories on social justice. Rawls believes social justice is to protect "equal basic rights and liberties and fair opportunities" of all citizens, as well as to address "the least advantaged" members of society (2001, p. 59). Equality is a critical element of social justice. "Equality means a fair distribution of each of the capacities needed to be normal and fully cooperating members of society over a complete life" (p. 8). Rawls's principles of equality can be a guidance for library services in order to build a good image in the community.

Miller's theory (2001) was built on public opinions and studies, and the theory focuses more on the context of a situation (pp. 62–63). Miller believes social justice influences the distribution of good (advantages) and bad (disadvantages) in society, as well as how they should be distributed in the society. Miller's theory addresses the concepts of need, desert, and equality. Need is defined as follows: when an individual is lacking in basic necessities, he or she is "being harmed or is in danger of being harmed and/or that one's capacity to function is being impeded" (p. 207, p. 210). Miller defined desert as the principle that one earns rewards based on performance, so that superior performance should be awarded with superior recognition (Miller, 2001, pp. 134, 141; Robinson, 2010, p. 9). *Stanford Encyclopedia of Philosophy* (Feldman, 2015) gives examples of the principle of desert, such as effort deserves success, innocent suffering deserves sympathy or compensation (http://plato.stanford.edu/entries/desert/). We achieve equality when society regards and treats its citizens equally and when benefits such as certain rights are distributed equally (Miller, 2001, p. 232). However there are certain groups within a society, and they are sometimes neglected.

Bonnici, Maatta, Wells, Brodsky, and Meadows (2012) emphasized that people who are physically challenged have the same information needs and intentions "to conduct their daily lives as those who are without disability" (p. 115). Using the typology of multiple qualifiers of social justice (Mehra, Albright, & Rioux, 2006), specifically, they concluded that libraries serving physically handicapped persons fall under the fairness and equity in social relationships in terms of "distributive justice," and incidental inequalities in the outcome do not arise. Under this perspective, the society should maximize the welfare of many, as even this practice comes at the expense of an innocent few (p. 118).

All of the theories from various disciplines mentioned above, such law, government, philosophy, and library science, can be used as guidelines for libraries to serve socially excluded residents. The following is part of a community outreach plan that demonstrates its effort to provide library services to socially excluded residents in the community:

> The library Books on Wheels outreach project is intended to provide reading or listening materials in a variety of formats to residents of Graham that are blind, disabled, homebound, or in long term care, regardless of age. When appropriate, the library will facilitate participation in programs such as Books Aloud, Inc., or Talking Books for those participating in Books on Wheels. The library will work with Graham ISD to identify students that might benefit from the service; Graham Senior Citizen Center Meals on Wheels to promote the service to people in their program, and Horizon Bay to advertise the service to residents there. (Gibson, 2011, p. 7)

Libraries, E-books, and Social Justice

Vincent (2012) argued that the general impression of a public library is more or less a building that lends books and the impact is often judged by numerical scores such as head counts or return on investment, but this method misses the important role that public libraries play in contributing toward social justice, the right that everyone has the chances and opportunities to make the most of their lives and to use their talent to the full (p. 351). A pure numerical assessment of head counts or return on investment ignores the needy and vulnerable, who are often small numbers of people, and steers librarians to provide library services to attract more and more people through the doors. When libraries offer support, information, and a connection to a wider community of people who are underserved and marginalized, they carry the mission of providing social justice for the society as a whole.

Social justice has been a concern in library services that use technologies. It is understandable that users with no Internet access can hardly keep updated with a library's e-mail newsletters. Furthermore, Molaro (2012), in his blog, complained of the price tag and circulation restrictions from e-book publishers and commented that the shift from print to digital content created an economic barrier to the access of information for many underprivileged citizens who simply cannot access the digital world or cannot afford to purchase e-books or e-readers. This barrier is becoming an issue of human rights, inequality, and social justice. It is a possibility that such barriers were created intentionally or unintentionally by humans. As American Library Association (1953) Freedom to Read Statement tells us:

> The freedom to read is essential to our democracy. It is continuously under attack. Private groups and public authorities in various parts of the country are working to remove or limit access to reading materials, to censor content in schools, to label "controversial" views, to distribute lists of "objectionable" books or authors, and to purge libraries. (http://www.ala.org/advocacy/intfreedom/statementspols /freedomreadstatement)

To better helping local residents' daily work, it is important to see that librarians are prepared with nonbias mindset and have developed culture awareness, which means "conscious attention to language or culture and, importantly, their engagement with these" (Byram, 2012, p. 6). At the same time, local residents need to be informed of local and national political events and be able to access nonbiased information through effective information seeking, cognitive information processing, and critical thinking skills (Smith, 2009).

Besides social justice, we will discuss social inclusion, another conceptual tool in public library practice.

SOCIAL INCLUSION

The World Bank (2015) defines social inclusion as "the process of improving the terms for individuals and groups to take part in society." It aims to assist underprivileged people have a "voice in decisions which affect their lives," and "to enjoy equal access to markets, services and political, social and physical spaces" (http://www.worldbank.org/en/topic/socialdevelopment/brief/ social-inclusion). Social inclusion is a more practical term in library services. Pateman and Vincent (2010) defined social inclusion as a paradigm in public library services that includes service to active users, passive (occasional) users, and nonusers through community engagement, and they suggested library usage may grow more if libraries make more of an effort to serve nonusers than passive and active users (p. 130). Pateman and Vincent (2010) also reviewed the history of the topic of social exclusion in public library service and warned that the term may have been expanded by political analysts referring to "healthcare reforms" or "faith-based activities." They also suggested that there is no ready measurement of social justice and recommended instead that researchers should look at the problem of inequality using the concepts of social inclusion and exclusion (p. 34). These concepts may help libraries to better serve all users, especially underserved populations. These include low-income families, homeless patrons, those in need of help accessing digital resources, socially excluded groups including senior citizens, immigrants who are cultural and linguistic minorities, and members of the community who need the Internet.

Low-Income Families and Homeless Persons

Public libraries have an important role in helping and serving low-income individuals and families. Among the underserved low-income groups, homeless patrons are a special group that often needs shelter, showers, and social services. Since nighttime shelters often close during daytime work hours, public spaces such as libraries become the first option for homeless people. Libraries provide safety, living conditions, and access to Internet to these socially excluded groups; however, these groups are often considered by many library staff members and patrons as disruptive, dangerous, and aggressive.

Anderson, Simpson, and Fisher (2012) cited the ALA 2011 policy manual that clearly states that the libraries and staff members need to "identify poor people's need and deliver relevant services" (p. 177). In their survey study, they found library staff members were aware of problems presented by homeless patrons and were willing to help these individuals, yet staff members were not well equipped to do so. Anderson et al. (2012) suggest that librarians to act as gatekeepers, an informal role as social workers who provide information and referrals to professional helpers.

Accessing the Digital Divide

Socially excluded populations often have fewer opportunities in the digital society due to the gap caused by digital divide. Norris (2001, p. 4) defined three aspects of the term digital divide: the *global divide* as "the divergence of Internet access between industrialized and developing societies"; the *social divide* concerning "the gap between information rich and poor in a nation"; and the *democratic divide* signified by the difference between "those who do, and do not, use the collection of digital resources to engage, mobilize, and participate in public life."

Social divide contributes to digital divide. For example, a Pew Research survey found that in the United States, adult cellphone ownership reached 91% by May 2013 but was lower among those who did not attend college, those living in household with an income of less than $30,000, those who are older, and those in rural areas (http://www.pewresearch.org/fact-tank/2013/06/06/cell-phone-ownership-hits-91-of-adults/). Only 85% of adults living in rural areas and only 76% of people 65 and older own a cell phone. Chapter 7 will discuss in detail on libraries bridging the digital divide.

Senior Citizens

Social-economic factors directly influence the ability to use library resources, making some potential patrons socially excluded. The philosophy of a library serving all community users freely is limited by the understanding that potential users have the ability and intention to use library facilities, either physically or virtually. Senior citizens who live in assisted-living facilities are extremely vulnerable to losing access to library services because these citizens may not be driving, and there are limited, if any, organized group visits to libraries.

Aging citizens living in retirement communities may experience isolation during their residency. As socioemotional selectivity theory suggests, when people grow older, they tend to "desire less social stimulation and novelty, and tend to select close, reliable relationships to meet their emotional needs" (Adams, Sanders, & Auth, 2004, p. 475). Social psychologists promote well-being as a living style with the "absence of negative conditions and feelings, the result of adjustment and adaption to a hazardous world" (Keyes, 1998, p. 121). Keyes also stated that as people grow older, they may encounter situations that require them to choose to remain isolated or adapt to become socially involved. This blend of private and public lifestyle may lead to a healthy, well-lived life, as the individual avoids from negative conditions and feelings, and one adjusts and adapts to a hazardous world. Libraries, traditionally centers of lifelong learning, often provide conditions of well-being through information services to seniors in the community and thus potentially enhance the quality of these citizens' lives, with offerings such as various reading clubs, intergenerational literacy programs, and other programs where different ages of readers can interact with each other (Moore, 2013).

Library outreach programs provide support to socially excluded groups due to aging and various physical limitations. People who shy away from using digital and handheld devices are excluded from today's digital society, and those who are not efficient at using computers find it hard to apply for jobs without using a computer or having an e-mail account. Multiple platforms and sizes of digital devices can confuse senior residents and, probably, linguistic minorities, who then shy away from using library e-books and electronic resources.

Serving Immigrants Who Are Cultural and Linguistic Minorities

According to the Pew Hispanic Center (2013), a project of the Pew Research Center, the United States' total immigrant population reached a record 40.4 million in 2011, and the number of unauthorized immigrants in the United States has grown from 8.4 million in 2000 to 11.1 million in 2011. Minorities whose first language is not English need libraries' services more since they face language barriers daily as they attempt to survive. If libraries lack staff members who have a similar background to that of the minorities, staff members will find difficulty to understand the minorities' information needs, information use, and information seeking behaviors. Unauthorized immigrants who don't have a library identification card or driver's license will find challenges when using library resources. New immigrants from developing countries may not realize that the library is free and may have concerns regarding the cost of using a library.

It is a challenging task for librarians to identify the information needs from various cultural and linguistic groups. They need to identify the groups they are targeting, for example children, teens, adults, families, or organizations in their community. To promote a broad awareness of services and materials that libraries have, libraries traditionally found themselves in an alliance with school districts and family literacy programs to provide language training or computer classes to new immigrants.

Members of the Community Who Need the Internet

The social divide is potentially widening between rural and affluent suburban and even urban areas, where more business capital and tax revenues are invested in information communication infrastructure. At the same time, the Internet has become increasing critical to education and job opportunities, and certain people are systematically excluded, such as poor and remote neighborhoods, minority or immigrant communities, and peripheral rural communities. It is important for libraries to include underserved populations in the digital world and embrace digital inclusion.

Digital inclusion is defined by Real, Bertot, and Jaeger (2014) as a framework through which one can understand the importance of ensuring that individuals have access to digital technologies as well as the means to learn how to use them (p. 8). Digital inclusion consists of policies and actions related to the digital divide and digital literacy. The digital divide is a gap between individuals who have readily available access to the Internet—oftentimes broadband Internet—and those don't. Digital literacy is the skill and knowledge related to language, hardware, and software needed in order to navigate and access digital information. Digital inclusion emphasizes policies and practices to provide digital access and outreach to underserved populations. Chapter 4 discusses more on broadband Internet access and digital divide.

One topic that is often overlooked by library fields is the less than adequate workforce in rural public libraries. An Institute of Museum and Library Services report (2013) indicated that the overall staffing level in rural libraries has decreased in recent years. The median number of librarians (full-time employee) is 1.0, and many of rural libraries do not have librarians working on a full-time schedule. Regardless of limited resources, many rural librarians provide excellent professional support to poor and remote neighborhoods, minorities and immigrants, and senior and homebound citizens who may need the Internet more for information access. The next section will discuss how professional ethics can serve as guidelines for social inclusion.

FREEDOM TO ACCESS INFORMATION

The principal of social inclusion mentioned in the previous section stems from the 1939 ALA Library Bill of Rights and, internationally, from the Universal Declaration of Human Rights (1948) by the United Nations (http://www.un.org/en/documents/udhr/). The ALA Library Bill of Rights is probably the most powerful professional tool to support library services to diverse users.

It was first adopted in 1939 by the ALA Council and amended in 1940s, 1960s, 1980s, and 1990s. The ALA Library Bill of Rights emphasizes that "books and other library resources should be provided for the interest, information, and enlightenment of all people of the community the library serves. Materials should not be excluded because of the origin, background, or views of those contributing to their creation" (American Library Association, 1996).

According to ALA, the principle of freedom to access also involves freedom to read and the principle of intellectual freedom, which is the opposite of censorship. Censorship, or information suppression, is the act of intentionally reducing free access to information, due to its controversial topics, nonmainstream topics, or unauthoritative opinions. Moody (2004) reported that there are three reasons for librarians to view materials as controversial: the content of the materials may "conflict with the librarian's personal values"; it may "violate perceived community standards"; or it may be "controversial as a result of the socio-political environment of the time." Where there is a conflict between a librarian's personal values and a user's information interest on a topic such as a particular sexual orientation or religious or political opinions, a librarian can potentially censor the information sources or avoid the information services that he or she could have provided. Librarians may choose to reduce a certain collection in order to satisfy a community conservation group or to just not offend anybody in the community. Free access to information may also be threatened under a particular social and political movement in which a library operates under at a certain point of time.

All these reasons mentioned above may lead to a small or rural librarian unintentionally selecting or censoring the materials to purchase for the library. Selection is primarily seeking reasons to include an item, while censoring looks for reasons to not to include an item. Librarians should use the professional ethics as a tool to defend themselves and focus on their job's responsibilities of providing the information sources rather than information content itself.

ALA also published its official interpretation of the Library Bill of Rights, available at its website (http://www.ala.org/advocacy/intfreedom/library bill/interpretations). Among these rights, one of the most important items is the access for children and young adults in libraries. While ALA recognized that the parents have the rights and responsibilities to restrict access of their children to library resources, it emphasizes the rights to use a library includes free and unrestricted access to all services and materials for children, since "a person's right to use a library should not be denied or abridged because of origin, age, background, or views." (American Library Association, 1996). For a small library, this core value of freedom to accesses information will ensure that a library serves all of its community users. The mission of the library is then changed from what the library wants to instead a role of facilitating the individuals' and community's growth. Such a valuable service, once promoted to the community, will make the library an essential asset of the community and will assist the library in gaining monetary and nonmonetary support.

ROLE OF LIBRARIES IN COMMUNITY USERS' LITERACY SKILLS

Information Poverty and Outsiders' Roles

Among the reports from library and information science (LIS) research on information access and poor communities, Chatman's (1996) theory on information poverty studied two groups of people regarding information use and sharing: insiders and outsiders. Insiders are members of the community that might have a common "cultural, social, religious" (p. 194) background and other life perspective. Insiders tend to keep themselves in an insulated, small worldview and share a sense that outsiders cannot understand a world different from their own, which leads to a condition of secrecy, deception, risk-taking, and self-protection during information exchange. The purpose of secrecy is to guard against disclosure and not to be receptive to advice or information. Deception means to hide an individual's real condition by sending out deceiving and misleading information. The purpose of secrecy and deception is to protect someone in a disadvantaged position or perceived potentially harmful condition. To Chatman, information poverty is the result of self-protective behaviors, in response to social norms.

In a rural library, if the director is hired from outside the community, he or she may be treated as an outsider by small town residents. In this case, the "outsider" taking one of the good jobs in the community can be considered a threat to the community. An internal hire, however, may be a compromise of local politics, but there is a chance that the library manager is not the best fit for the position. Furthermore, a new library director as an outsider might be the case when there is a digital divide between affluent communities and poorer communities, where not only information infrastructure is limited but also the residents in these communities may choose not to disclose their conditions to outsiders. This might include new library directors who must learn to acculturate to a new working condition and try to be one of the "insiders," but these directors will be often excluded by local politics. To break the ice and fit the local culture, a new library director may build stronger ties with a community through initiating and expanding library services and reaching out to various users, including labor communities, immigrants, and linguistic minorities.

Library Service to Local Labor Force

In history, the primary beneficiary of Americans' free public library system has been the American workers. Since the early days of the nation, libraries have traditionally held various forms of outreach, including programming and cooperative services designed specifically for workers, and many of the programs were in cooperation with the labor movement (Sparanese, 2002). Today, one of the fastest growing labor forces is foreign-born immigrants ages 5 years and over, who reached 40.6 million in 2012 (Gambino, Acosta, & Grieco, 2014).

The American Community Survey by the U.S. Census Bureau found that among the foreign-born population, 84.6% speak a language other than English at home (p. 2).

Changes in immigration demographics suggest that libraries should serve the information needs of new and emerging labor forces, particularly new immigrants and their children. At the same time, libraries continue to carry the mission to enhance the local workforce in various formats, such as reading and computer literacy skills. The concept of literacy is not limited to traditional reading and writing skills but also includes computer literacy and media literacy (Mackey, 2007). Libraries and their resources allow community users to develop fluency in their information skills including reading literacy.

> We know of print processing that a highly important step in the acquisition of skills and abilities is the development of automaticity. We need to be able to recognize almost every word, effortlessly and instantly. As long as our attention is focused on decoding individual words, we do not have attention to spar to be able to make meaning of the text as a whole. If you have ever heard a beginning reader laboriously process even a short passage of text, stopping every word or two to decipher what on earth could be coming next, you will know how meaning-deficient the final result can be. (Mackey, 2007, p. 88)

Librarians often find themselves teaching the local labor force, especially new immigrants, basic computer literacy skills so that they can use e-mail systems and apply for jobs online. The use of digital and the Internet media is becoming a necessary survival skill in today's social environment, and virtually all job applications are online. Handheld technologies such as smartphones and iPads also change personal entertainment from TV and print media to Internet-based digital media and social media. The training needed from the labor force requires librarians to maintain and update their technology skills constantly.

Libraries and Literacy Programs

Chu (1999) emphasized that literacy, as it is applies to linguistic minorities, needs to be understood "as a discourse of power" (p. 339) and must be redefined "for librarians to provide appropriate services" (p. 344). She suggested that "basic or technical definitions of literacy are concerned with the acquisition of literacy skills, that is, reading, writing, and speaking a language" (p. 343), and some even only narrowly mean English skills; some aspect of literacy refer to the ability to "analyze and critically evaluate information," or "information literacy" (p. 344). However, a person who may not know English may be literate in his/her own language and can still survive and sustain as long as there is a support network from the same culture background, so that the person can depend on the ties of his/her own background in the adoptive country.

Another concept, digital literacy, represents one's ability to complete tasks effectively in a digital environment. Digital literacy includes "the ability to read and interpret media (text, sound, images), to reproduce data and images through digital manipulation, and to evaluate and apply new knowledge gained from digital environments" (Jones-Kavalier & Flannigan, 2006, p. 9).

To build library literacy programs, potential targets' literacy levels in the heritage language, education attainment, presence of an ethnic community, degree of social isolation, and connections are all factors to be considered. To understand the true literacy level of linguistic minorities is a challenge to many librarians, since self-reported data are unreliable. Grade level achievement may not totally represent skills learned in the workplace or community. Even direct access has potential problems if the user does not fully understand the questions in English. Chu (1999) suggested literacy programs should start with the participants' native or heritage languages and use content and teaching methods that are "culturally relevant to the participants" (p. 355). Libraries should also collaborate with partners such as businesses and government entities, as well as local institutions offering educational, religious, and social services.

Public libraries often offer English as a second language (ESL) programs or provide space for ESL groups to meet regularly. The classes are often taught by retired teachers and are offered free of charge to foreign-born students. Libraries often actively seek grants or collaborate with local partners to have the financial resources needed in order to support to teachers and programs. Libraries provide a learning environment that leads to meeting and socializing with people with similar cultural backgrounds sharing the experience of learning English. This socializing venue is important to scaffold a positive learning environment.

Supporting Homeschooling and GED or High School Diplomas

No definite number is available for how many students age 5 to 17 (a grade equivalent of kindergarten to 12th grade) are homeschooled. The U.S. National Center for Education Statistics estimated there were 1.5 million home-schooled students in 2007 (Bielick, 2008). Brian Ray (2011), president of the National Home Education Research Institute, reported that there are 2.04 million homeschool students in the United States.

Different states have different regulations. According to Home School Legal Defense Association (https://www.hslda.org/LAWS/default.asp), some states, such as New York and Pennsylvania, are very strict. They require parents to send notifications and student achievement scores and even accept home visits by state officials, while some states, such as Illinois, Michigan, and Texas, have very few requirements for the curriculum. For example, in Texas, the curriculum only needs to include the five basic subjects of "reading, spelling, grammar, mathematics, and good citizenship" (Texas Home School Coalition Association, n.d.).

For many homeschoolers, preparing for a General Educational Development (GED) test may require extra work. Passing GED tests will certify one with an equivalent to high school-level academic skills, and jobs require a GED.

GED testing is administered by American Council on Education (http://www
.acenet.edu/). GED examinations consist of five divided skills: language arts
(writing), social studies, science, language arts (reading), and mathematics.

As lifelong learning centers in their communities, rural public libraries are natural partners to homeschooling families (http://publiclibrariesonline
.org/2014/04/the-perfect-partnership-public-libraries-and-homeschoolers/). The
library staff in Loudoun County Public Library in Virginia, while collaborating with homeschool parents and teachers, created Homeschool Enrichment
classes, including Library Skills for Homeschoolers. The classes were huge success and made positive impact to the community (Hunter, 2014).

Another example is the Bertha Voyer Memorial Library in Honey
Grove, Texas, which we have mentioned in chapter 2. It also has a successful
ESL and GED courses and various other programs throughout the year (http://
www.kxii.com/home/headlines/Honey-Grove-library-is-nationally-recognized
-254058411.html). The examples above demonstrate that small libraries can
make big impact in their communities.

CONCLUSION

Libraries serving community users equally is a concept that is based on
the principle of social justice, and the profession has been providing inclusive
service and programming to low-income families, senior citizens, immigrants,
and linguistic minorities. Small and rural libraries offering literacy programs
are fostering social justice and social inclusion, and they help linguistic minorities become full participants in the development, implementation, and evaluation of library literacy programs and move up the social-economic ladder.

Understanding the concept of social justice may help new library managers to understand the culture of the town if he or she is an outsider of the town,
to better prepare to defend the freedom to access information, and to provide
literacy programs in the community, all of which are essential for people to succeed in today's digital world. Libraries providing literacy programs can reduce
information poverty and make a big impact in their communities. Chapter 4 will
introduce more on social transition in rural libraries.

REFERENCES

Adams, K. B., Sanders, S., & Auth, E. A. (2004). Loneliness and depression in independent living retirement communities: Risk and resilience factors. *Aging and Mental
Health*, 8(6), 475–485.

American Library Association. (1953). *The freedom to read statement*. Chicago,
IL: American Library Association. Available at http://www.ala.org/advocacy
/intfreedom/statementspols/freedomreadstatement

American Library Association. (1996). *Library Bill of Rights.* Chicago, IL: American Library Association. Available at http://www.ala.org/advocacy/intfreedom/librarybill

Anderson, K. A., Simpson, C. D., & Fisher, L. G. (2012). The ability of public library staff to help homeless people in the United States: Exploring relationships, roles and potential. *Journal of Poverty and Social Justice, 20*(2), 177–190.

Bielick, S. (2008). 1.5 million homeschooled students in the United States in 2007. Washington, DC: U.S. Department of Education (National Center for Education Statistics). Available at http://nces.ed.gov/pubs2009/2009030.pdf

Bonnici, L. J., Maatta, S. L., Wells, M. K., Brodsky, J., & Meadows, C. W. III. (2012). Physiological access as a social justice type in LIS curricula. *Journal of Education for Library and Information Science, 53*(2), 115–129.

Byram, M. (2012). Language awareness and (critical) cultural awareness—relationships, comparison and contrasts. *Language Awareness, 21*(1/2), 5–13.

Chatman, E. (1996). The impoverished life-world of outsiders. *Journal of American Society for Information Science, 47*(3), 193–206.

Chu, C. (1999). Literacy practices of linguistic minorities: Sociolinguistic issues and implications for literacy services. *Library Quarterly, 39*(3), 339–359.

Feldman, F. (2015). Desert. In E. N. Zalta (Ed.), *Stanford encyclopedia of philosophy.* Stanford, CA: Stanford University. Available at http://plato.stanford.edu/entries/desert/

Gambino, C. P., Acosta, Y. D., & Grieco, E. M. (2014). English-speaking ability of the foreign-born population in the United States: 2012 American community survey reports [Data file]. Available at http://www.census.gov/content/dam/Census/library/publications/2014/acs/acs-26.pdf

Gibson, S. (2011). *Library of Graham community outreach plan.* Denton, TX: PEARL Project, University of North Texas. Available at https://pearl.unt.edu/sites/default/files/libraryofgram.pdf

Hunter, C. (2014). The perfect partnership: Public libraries and homeschoolers. *Public Libraries Online.* Chicago, IL: Public Library Association. Available at http://publiclibrariesonline.org/2014/04/the-perfect-partnership-public-libraries-and-homeschoolers/

Institute of Museum and Library Services (2013). *The state of small and rural libraries in the United States* (Research Brief No. 5, September 2013). Washington, DC: Institute of Museum and Library Services. Available at https://www.imls.gov/assets/1/AssetManager/Brief2013_05.pdf

Jones-Kavalier, B. R., & Flannigan, S. L. (2006). Connecting the digital dots: Literacy of the 21st century. *EDUCAUSE Quarterly, 29*(2), 8–10. Available at http://www.educause.edu/ero/article/connecting-digital-dots-literacy-21st-century

Keyes, C. L. (1998). Social well-being. *Social Psychology Quarterly, 61*(2), 121–140.

Mackey, M. (2007). Mapping recreational literacies: Contemporary adults at play. New York, NY: Peter Lang.

Mehra, B., Albright, K. S., & Rioux, K. (2006). A practical framework for social justice research in the information professions. *Proceedings of the American Society for Information Science and Technology, 43*(1), 1–10.

Miller, D. (2001). *Principles of social justice.* Cambridge, MA: Harvard University Press.

Molaro, A. (2012). eBooks, human rights and social justice [Blog post]. Available at http://informationactivist.com/2012/04/09/ebooks-human-rights-and-social-justice/

Moody, K. (2004). Censorship by Queensland public librarians: Philosophy and practice. *APLIS 17*(4), 168–185.

Moore, C. (2013). Intergenerational programming at your library [Blog post]. Available at http://www.alsc.ala.org/blog/2013/05/intergenerational-programming-at-your-library/

Norris, P. (2001). *Digital divide: Civic engagement, information poverty, and the Internet worldwide.* Cambridge, United Kingdom: Cambridge University Press.

Pateman, J., & Vincent, J. (2010). *Public libraries and social justice.* Farnham, United Kingdom: Ashgate.

Pew Hispanic Center. (2013). *A nation of immigrants.* Washington, DC: Pew Research Center. Available at http://www.pewhispanic.org/2013/01/29/a-nation-of-immigrants/

Rawls, J. (2001). *Justice as fairness: A restatement.* Cambridge, MA: Harvard University Press.

Ray, B. (2011). *2.04 million homeschool students in the United States in 2010.* Salem, OR: National Home Education Research Institute. Available at https://www.nheri .org/HomeschoolPopulationReport2010.pdf

Real, B., Bertot, J. C., & Jaeger, P. T. (2014). Rural public libraries and digital inclusion: Issues and challenges. *Information Technology and Libraries, 33*(1), 6–24.

Rioux, K. S. (2010). Metatheory in library and information science: A nascent social justice approach. *Journal of Education for Library and Information Science, 51*(1), 8–16.

Rioux, K. S., Mehra, B., & Albright, K. (2007). Conceptualizing social justice in the information sciences. *Proceedings of the Annual Meeting of the American Society for Information Science and Technology, 44*(1), 1–4.

Robinson, M. B. (2010). Assessing criminal justice practice using social justice theory. *Social Justice Research, 23,* 77–97.

Shields, L. W. (1941). The history and meaning of the term social justice (Doctoral dissertation, University of Note Dame). Available at http://archive.org/stream /historymeaningof00shie/historymeaningof00shie_djvu.txt

Smith, L. (2009). Building social justice through library and information science. Unpublished Paper from Academia.edu. San Francisco: CA. Available at http://www .academia.edu/2961931/Building_social_justice_through_library_and_information _science

Sparanese, A. C. (2002). Service to the labor community: A public library perspective. *Library Trends, 51*(1), 19–35.

Texas Home School Coalition Association. (n.d.). State requirements. Lubbock, TX: Texas Home School Coalition Association. Available at http://www.thsc.org/homeschooling -in-texas/state-requirements/

The United Nations. (1948). *The universal declaration of human rights.* New York: The United Nations. Available at http://www.un.org/en/universal-declaration-human -rights/index.html

Vincent, J. (2012). The role of public libraries in social justice. *Prometheus: Critical Studies in Innovation, 30*(3), 349–351.

The World Bank. Social inclusion. Washington, DC: The World Bank. Available at http://www.worldbank.org/en/topic/socialdevelopment/brief/social-inclusion

CHAPTER FOUR

Effecting Social Transition

While academic and urban libraries may have larger pools of talent to fill various positions, rural public libraries often have to recruit from a very small pool of local candidates. These may be retired teachers or persons with little more than a high school education or two years of college. When a community is lucky, they may find someone with business management skills. New rural library directors, even those with the master of library and information science (MLIS) degree, usually experience frequent community and social transitions during their adjustment from being a library outsider to the manager of the library. Social transition in this chapter stands for the changing fiscal, political, and community environments that the library staff faces. It sometimes involves struggling with the community and its voters and other constituents. It also requires a great deal of effort to reach the library's funders and other stakeholders such as city managers, mayors, county judges, and so on.

This chapter addresses social transition in four topics: the changing role of the library, transitioning as a new library director, the library and broadband Internet, and digital training for librarians in rural and small libraries. We will begin with the changing role of the library.

LIBRARY'S ROLE CHANGE

A wealth of research is available on the social roles of libraries in terms of their economic, educational, and social impact to their communities. Libraries support the literacy of their diverse residents, add value to their neighborhoods, advance learning and personal development, and aim to be a safe gathering place for communities. (http://www.ala.org/research/librariesmatter /taxonomy/term/143). To adjust to the library's changing roles in communities, new librarians should prepare for their role change and be ready to adapt from an information consumer to a leader, educator, and social worker in their communities.

The Role of Libraries in Neighborhoods

As mentioned in chapter 2, the value of libraries can be judged by the numbers of patrons they serve and the economic value they bring, and there are survey studies reporting the plausible direct return on investment (ROI) on libraries. For example, in the Minnesota study funded by Institute of Museum and Library Services (IMLS), the rate ROI is calculated by per capita contribution of libraries divided by per capita tax support. The total economic contribution of libraries contains areas such as programs for children and young adults, circulation, public Internet access, and reference transactions, among others; these areas are multiplied by per attendance value, or the circulation per item value, in order to calculate the ROI (University of Minnesota Duluth, 2011, p. 52). The Minnesota study found for every dollar in support of Minnesota's public libraries, the ROI is estimated at $4.62.

The direct economic value can be a good indicator to demonstrate how public libraries improve quality of life and how well tax money is used, and these can be presented very well for rural and small library funders. However, other aspects of a library's roles, such as libraries improving the quality of community life and the use of public libraries for community involvement, are probably as important as the direct benefits. They are not easily quantifiable, but they should be understood by library directors and be promoted to related parties in the communities. To understand the intangible values, one should investigate library services and relevant parties.

The Role of Libraries to Stakeholders

Public libraries need to promote their roles to related parties during the process of assessing value-added services. These parties are stakeholders, or "people engaged in value creation and trade are responsible precisely to 'those groups and individuals who can affect or be affected by their actions'" (Freeman, Harrison, Wicks, Parmar, & De Colie, 2010, p. 9). The same Minnesota study cited above (University of Minnesota Duluth, 2011, p. 59) also defined public library stakeholders as "inside and outside the library represent(ing) library users with children or grandchildren; employees from the community at large, who check out materials for use at their workplace, as well as job seekers; library users who contact public library reference libraries for information; and technology users with a need for Internet access" (http://www.ala .org/research/librariesmatter/node/594). Identifying library stakeholders can help a library to advocate its programs and efforts to those who directly benefit from them and recognize those who are likely to cheer for the steps that the library takes.

The value of library services can be demonstrated through benefits to both its primary and secondary stakeholders. The American Library Association (ALA) division, Association for Library Services to Children (ALSC), proposed that primary stakeholders are those who benefit directly from its services, such as children, parents and their surrogates, educational partners, organizations serving youth, and so on, and secondary stakeholders are individuals or groups who may not reap the immediate benefits but who share the mission for supporting the families in the community; for example, people of influence in the community, local government administrators, local business people, local support groups, cultural and nonprofit organizations, and funders and philanthropic individuals and groups are all secondary stakeholders. Using or not-using library services, the educational value of library service is undeniable.

Educational values are also represented by individuals using library facilities as gathering places, due to their abundant learning resources. The "gathering place," a phenomenon known as the "living room" experience, is an area not often discussed as the library's value. Libraries provide free meeting and conference rooms in a friendly environment and are a unique location for community residents to socialize, attend classes, participate in literacy instruction, and formulate book clubs and reading groups, as well as a safe place where people can sit, talk, read, and express their interests and concerns. It is an ideal setting for cultural and leisure activities to take place in the local community. As a place where people from different socioeconomic statuses and cultural backgrounds can use the library resources freely, libraries have the potential to help people from low-income families to climb the academic and professional ladder and reach personal goals. Librarians, particularly those who are new to rural communities, should understand the library's changing role, from an information access point to value-added public services, either tangible or intangible. Moreover, the library's value as perceived in their own community can serve as a guideline to assess the library's performance as well as an aid in gaining broader support.

The person who is responsible for presenting the role of the library to the community is the library director. As stated earlier in the chapter, this may not be an easy process.

HIRING A RURAL LIBRARY DIRECTOR

Recruiting rural library directors is sometimes not easy, as many rural libraries are far from city centers. In some instances staff members may be available because of an unusual work experience for the potential librarian's spouse. When employment opportunities require a spouse to relocate, the other spouse, looking for meaningful employment may think that running the library is just such a position. However, those people who think that all a librarian has to do is check out books will need to have some explanation of the complexities of the position. Sometimes this can be a part of the job description in the ad for the position.

Many published resources are available to learn more about the common expectations for such job titles. The Association for Rural and Small Libraries (ARSL), for example, often publishes such job advertisements on their website (http://arsl.info/), as well as the state library websites—see, for example, the one from North Carolina (http://statelibrary.ncdcr.gov/ld/jobs.html); there is even an ALA job listing website that may occasionally post small library jobs (http://joblist.ala.org/). The following is part of the posted job advertisements from ARSL website in July, 2015:

> The Library Director is responsible for the daily operations of the main library in [city name] and a small branch library in [city name], including administration, programs, customer service, and marketing. The Director will also be essential in developing a vision for the newly renovated and expanded library's future. (http://arsl.info/category/jobs/)

Just as the job advertisement above indicated, rural library directors are often expected to have a well-rounded skillset necessary to solving various problems independently, with ability to communicate with technical consultants for problem solving too. This may be caused by the limited financial resources and limited technical support available in rural and small communities. Due to the limited financial support that a rural community can afford, a master of library science (MLS) degree is not always required for small library director positions. The following is another example of a job advertisement:

> We are looking for an enthusiastic, capable individual with both creative vision and the skills to bring the vision into reality. This person will enjoy problem-solving, multi-tasking, providing high-quality customer service and programs to people of all sorts and representing the library in the community.

Library directors are the face of the library, representing their library in their small community, even when they are not at work but on their own time. This constant pressure of being under the spotlight means a rural librarian needs to be an advocate for library services at all times, whether in the work-place or in the community. Librarians must always be prepared to engage with the community and with their library users and potential users. The University of North Texas Promoting & Enhancing the Advancement of Rural Libraries (UNT PEARL) Project (pearl.unt.edu) found that many rural librarians were recruited in the career field by random factors, and this means that they may face tremendous challenges when they start, including limited budgets, out-of-date library collections, and sometimes pressure from the senior staff with connections in the local communities.

Some communities may decide not to recruit library professionals and decide to instead hire a local person with strong local connections. New library leaders without professional training may feel overwhelmed by the pressure of their new positions.

TRANSITION AS A NEW LIBRARIAN

Once the new librarian is hired, a transition period is often needed to adjust to the work procedures. This section discusses job transition and resources for new librarians.

Job Transition

In her book, *The NextGen Librarian's Survival Guide*, Rachel Singer Gorden (2006) pointed out that when new librarians begin their careers, they will have new concerns. New librarians have to learn to survive in an environment, often one with bureaucratic systems that are resistant to change, or a workplace with little institutional support. Sometimes they may be lucky to be surrounded by more experienced and older professionals. However, in some locations, they may be the only librarian at the facility with no one to help. This is particularly true in small or rural libraries, where the budget and human resources are constant concerns.

While new library directors of these small or rural libraries might need a period of adjustment, this may be a luxury they do not have. They may be hired immediately after a job turnover and be put in a position to meet tough deadlines, finding themselves responsible for making an annual library budget or year-end financial report or even expected to implement changes in technologies. Since many reports need data to be collected ahead of time and even over a number of years, new directors have to find supportive environments and resources to help them jumpstart their career.

To make the transition to a new rural library position, a candidate needs to scan the environment and learn what is expected in the market. Due to limited budget, in many such positions, librarians are expected to work solo, thus the position often requires multiple skills. Some positions even expect the librarian to work at different physical buildings during the same week.

Faced with a new position in a library where there is no other professional staff, the newly appointed librarian who needs help can look for it in a nearby library. Another source of assistance would be a local, regional, or state library network.

LIBRARY NETWORKS

One of the best resources for a new library director is the regional library network. For example, in Lubbock, Texas, the Harrington Library Consortium is a nonprofit organization comprising school, academic, and public libraries from 38 nearby cities (http://harringtonlc.org/hlc-directory/). Member libraries receive various benefits from the system, such as consulting and continuing education services, as well as literacy and technology projects. Regional library networks, such as library systems, enable librarians to network and share information, expertise, and resources, and many of these facilities join a library consortium in order to save costs on acquisition and digital resources.

If a state does not have a regional network, librarians in small and rural libraries have access to their state library staff members who will provide assistance when they are called. Many of these state libraries offer training for any librarian who can attend the training session. Another solution is that more and more social networking tools are used by librarians. Communication tools such as Facebook, Twitter, and LinkedIn allow librarians from remote areas to connect to the field and receive the latest updates in very short period of time.

Perhaps the most efficient way to set up a network of librarians within the state is to attend the state library association annual conference. When this is possible, a network can be established to help answer questions. It may be that one of the first actions after being appointed is to find a nearby library and form a library network.

LIBRARY AND BROADBAND INTERNET

The advent of technology and the possibilities that come with adding technology to your library may be one to the greatest challenges to a new library director in a small or rural library. The choices that must be made are professional ones, and they usually have an influence on the budget.

Inequity of Broadband Coverage

According to census data, 20% of the U.S. population lives in rural areas or communities with populations fewer than 25,000, but rural areas cover 84% of U.S. territories (United States Census Bureau, 2010). Unlike other populated areas, the information infrastructure, particular broadband Internet, is still underdeveloped in rural America. Broadband is provided by a series of technologies (e.g., cable, telephone wire, fiber, satellite, wireless) that give users the ability to send and receive data at volumes and speeds far greater than traditional "dial-up" Internet access over telephone lines (Kruger & Gilroy, 2013). The national broadband map ("National Broadband Map," 2013) data shows large portions of the United States with no connection with broadband Internet via digital subscriber line (DSL), cable, and fiber optic (Broadbandmap.gov). The broadband map also shows that most U.S. territories are covered under wireless mobile Internet connections, but the price tag of a mobile data plan is obvious prohibitive to most rural residents.

According to Henderson (2009), rural communities need technology-related support such as a broadband Internet connection, computers, and electronic resources. Pew Internet and American Life Project (Smith, 2010) concluded that the majority of people with no broadband access are people with low incomes, seniors, minorities, those who are less educated, those in nonfamily households, and those who are nonemployed. Families that do not have broadband Internet also perceive it as not necessary or too expensive or lack an updated computer. The Eighth Broadband Progress Report found 19 million Americans (6% of the population) still lack access to fixed broadband service at threshold speeds; among them, 14.5 million people are from rural areas, or one-fourth of the rural population. In tribal areas, nearly one-third of the population lacks broadband access. Even in areas where broadband is available, approximately 100 million Americans still do not subscribe (https://www .fcc.gov/reports/eighth-broadband-progress-report).

In recent years, federal support has increased for rural library facilities and technology-related personnel training. Such increased support has the potential to change the daily lives in rural and remote areas, increase the quality of life, and make the transition of rural libraries and information centers more social.

An example of federally funded projects in rural communities is the Broadband Technology Opportunities Program (BTOP) by the National Telecommunications and Information Administration (NTIA). Through the BTOP program, libraries are becoming public computer centers and providing Internet access to the public, and libraries can "improve the online learning experience and even allow interactive classes" (Thibodeau, 2010, p. 15). Furthermore, the United States Department of Agriculture has been funding the construction or remodeling of rural library buildings through loans and grants, and the IMLS has supported both educational programs and projects to provide broadband facilities in rural libraries. IMLS held a public hearing in April 2014 and suggested that broadband enhances local economic development and helps residents train themselves and seek job opportunities online. IMLS also reported on the success of libraries and schools taking advantage of E-rate, a subsidized Internet program, and on the linking of communities to the outside world.

Rural Libraries as Community Information Anchors

Studies suggest information technology infrastructure may greatly empower the role of libraries in rural communities as technology centers. Alemanne, Mandel, and McClure (2011) commended rural libraries' new role as the "anchor of anchors" that might fund the rural library continuously and sustain the service to rural communities (p. 20). They suggested librarians and information professionals have the knowledge, credibility, visibility, and community in their communities. Such a great amount of community trust may enable rural libraries to transform from traditional book lending places to community learning centers, knowledge hubs, and technology stakeholders in rural communities. As the same time, information infrastructures will enable libraries to perform traditional information roles such as helping the community with access to e-government, economic development, information technology training, and online job applications.

The Universal Service Program for Schools and Libraries, also known as the E-rate program, provides discounted telecommunications, Internet access, and internal connection to eligible schools and libraries. Mandated by Congress in 1996, and implemented by the Federal Communications Commission (FCC) in 1997, the E-rate provides discounted telecommunications, Internet access, and internal connections to eligible schools and libraries, funded by the Universal Service Fund (USF). The discount ranges from 20% to 90%, depending on poverty level and remoteness of the institution, but schools or libraries always cost-share at least part of the cost of service (http://www.fcc.gov/guides/universal-service-program-schools-and-libraries). The FCC stated the following on their website:

> The FCC's E-rate program connects the nation's schools and libraries to broadband. It is the government's largest educational technology program. When E-rate was established in 1996, only 14 percent of the nation's K-12 classrooms had access to the Internet. Today, virtually all schools and libraries have Internet access. (United States Federal Communications Commission, 2015a)

E-rate provided libraries more than $250 million in technology and services by libraries and consortia from 2000 to 2004 alone (Jeager, McClure, & Bertot, 2005). ALA also reported that "the E-rate has helped change the public library's information technology landscape," as well as assists U.S. libraries to offer free Internet and Wi-Fi services to the public (American Library Association, n.d.).

While small and rural libraries offer free Internet access to community users, there are limitations for them to fully reach their full potential. The first obstacle is digital disparities between rural libraries as well as urban or suburban ones. Real, Bertot, and Jaeger (2014) stated that 70.3% of rural libraries are the only free Internet and computer terminal access providers in their service communities, compared with 40.6% of urban and 60.0% suburban libraries. This might be caused by the cost and difficulty of building communication infrastructure in less populated areas. As mentioned in chapter 1, the Bill & Melinda Gates Foundation will be ending their support of libraries. Since 1997, the Gates Foundation has invested $1 billion in its mission to provide Internet access in libraries worldwide and supported 13,000 public libraries in almost 20 countries. In 2011, it funded $12 million in grants to U.S. public libraries (Chant, 2014). Operating systems and software updates occur every year, and new computers become obsolete in a few years. Rural libraries have not been able to stay up-to-date. They typically have older computers, slower Internet, and less support from the federal government, and at the same time, in recent years, there is an increased growth of local demand for Internet use and technological training for job seekers.

Not enough literature is published on small libraries serving rural communities. Harding (2008) searched published literature on information literacy instruction and found that the research reports were mainly focused on school or academic environments. This probably makes public librarians, particularly those at small libraries, consider information literacy skill training not the focus of their work. Flatley and Wyman (2009) surveyed rural public libraries and found that 80% of them have a single full-time employee, and 50% have two or fewer paid employees. At the same time, 14% of these employees earned an MLS degree, 32% have a bachelor's degree, and 37% completed only a high school diploma. This seems to be one of the major reasons rural libraries are not able to offer technology training to their community users, hence aggravating the digital exclusion of rural communities, regardless of a user's age, gender, or ethnicity differences.

Digital Inclusion and Broadband Coverage

As stated earlier in this chapter, in addition to being community information anchors, rural and small libraries often find themselves to be the only place for community for users to access the Internet and reduce the digital gap with more affluent communities. Using high speed Internet to access the technology and new Web 2.0 media and understanding terminologies for computer hardware and software are increasing necessary digital literacy skills today. Many public rural libraries' efforts on computer training to the general public included using basic computers, using e-mail, and accessing the Internet. Hoffman, Bertot, and Davis (2012) found 77.3% of rural libraries offer informal point-of-use assistance on technologies, and only 25.2% report offering formal training classes. IMLS research suggested hardware development, such as broadband Internet access, is the foundation of embracing digital inclusion to the underserved population. Digital inclusion addresses individuals' and groups' access to and use of information and communication technologies. "Digital inclusion encompasses not only access to the Internet but also the availability of hardware and software; relevant content and services; and training for the digital literacy skills required for effective use of information and communication technologies" (Institute of Museum and Library Services, 2012, p. 1).

The first step in estimating the impact of broadband Internet on digital inclusion and better community life is to measure broadband coverage, such wire line capacity at basic speeds, and mobile wireless access. Connected Nation's Broadband Readiness Index uses the National Telecommunications and Information Administration's National Broadband Map county data to focus on three key metrics: wire line capacity at basic speeds, mobile wireless access, and high-capacity speeds greater than 50 Mbps (Connected Nation, 2011).

The FCC recently mandated broadband speed to be at least 10 Mbps download/1Mbps upload speed, in order to incentivize the rural broadband providers to bid on the funding of the projects on Connect America. (http://www.eweek.com/networking/fcc-boosts-rural-broadband-speed-requirements-to-10-mbps.html). Currently, the FCC has allocated $100 million for its rural broadband experiments in the next 10 years (http://www.fcc.gov/encyclopedia/rural-broadband-experiments).

Connect America stated this:

> Broadband has gone from being a luxury to a necessity for full participation in our economy and society—for all Americans. For that reason, the FCC has adopted comprehensive reforms of its Universal Service Fund (USF) and Intercarrier Compensation (ICC) systems to accelerate broadband build-out to the 15 million Americans living in rural areas who currently have no access to robust broadband infrastructure. (United States Federal Communications Commission, 2015b)

Community-Based Broadband Modeling

A model that incorporates factors of community attributes and community needs is the Community-Based Broadband Measuring Index by Carmichael, McClure, Mandel, and Mardis (2012, p. 2454). In this model, four factors are considered: community base, community-based needs assessment, community-based planning and deployment, and outcomes assessment. Mandel, Alemanne, and McClure (2012) also suggested that situational factors may impact broadband adoption in terms of both enablers and barriers, which include administrative support, funding, broadband availability, and knowledge on broadband. This seems to be a plausible model in research that looks at the impact of broadband Internet on community life and transition.

The Public Library & Broadband survey in 2014, conducted by the ALA and the University of Maryland, as part of Digital Inclusion Survey, revealed that nearly 40% of libraries have the Internet download speed between 1.6 and 10 Mbps, while nearly 10% libraries' Internet is below 1.5Mbps (See http://digitalinclusion.umd.edu/sites/default/files/BroadbandIssueBrief2014.pdf). The survey also reported that public libraries consider the cost and maximum speed available as two of the most significant challenges they face in order to improve the technology and access.

Currently, the White House published a paper promoting community-based broadband solutions in order to reduce legal barriers in 16 states, restricting local municipalities from building and expanding their broadband services (https://www.whitehouse.gov/sites/default/files/docs/community-based_broadband_report_by_executive_office_of_the_president.pdf). However, much is to be debated as to whether local government is in an advantageous position when competing with private enterprise. At the same time, bigger private communication companies are suspicious of monopoly and also restrict the competition. The result of the ongoing legal battle in 2015 between the FCC and the states of Tennessee and North Carolina might have a great influence on rural broadband (http://www.cnet.com/news/fcc-supersedes-state-laws-limiting-local-run-broadband-in-two-states/).

Even with the compensation of E-rate, funding a broadband Internet connection is a constant challenge for rural and small libraries. Currently, the majority of the funding to rural libraries is from local and private donations, and little is from the federal level. Broadband is one kind of a basic communication infrastructure, and it is hard to use the general maintenance budget to support these projects. It requires federal, state level, and even local government infrastructure investments.

DIGITAL LITERACY AND TRAINING IN RURAL AND SMALL LIBRARIES

However, the library's increased responsibility for literacy training reflects the community's needs, and this may lead the library to become an essential part of education centers in the community. Rural public libraries are as important as school districts, fire stations, police forces, and so on. They are traditionally recognized as places of lifelong learning, and they serve the information needs of diverse members of the community, with the potential to reach from children to seniors and from immigrants to long-term residents. Libraries are the first learning experience for children via story time and youth programs. More important, rural libraries are often the only place in the community that has broad connections available for local residents. Small and rural public libraries provide valuable opportunities to labor community users on information skills training, including computer skills, e-mail support, Internet use, searching, and job applications, as well as literacy skills such as English as second language, book talks and book clubs, a reader's advisory, and other children and young adults literacy services; even after these values have been acknowledge, many of them are still often short of staff members and resources.

The infrastructures and technology improvements are the emerging needs of residents in rural areas facing the digital age. To make greater social impacts to community transitions, rural librarians actively provide digital literacy training to community users. The ALA Digital Inclusion survey reported 86.5% of public libraries provide classes to the public on computer use, the Internet, and wireless Internet use. They also provide resources on digital health information (http://digitalinclusion.umd.edu/sites/default/files/DigitalLiteracyIssueBrief 2014.pdf).

Participants of the UNT PEARL Project completed their community outreach plan, which are available at the PEARL Project website. Some of the outreach plans are digital literacy classes for community users. This is one of the examples:

> The library plans to implement a four-week Basic Computer Skills Workshop for Adults. The program will acquaint those with little or no computer skills with the parts and applications of personal computers. The course will cover keyboarding, mouse skills, emailing, basic word processing, and Internet searching. The classes will be held in October and meet once per week on Monday evenings from 7:00 p.m. to 8:00 p.m. The classes will be held in the library, and will be limited to seven participants. This is a pilot project to gauge the level of interest and need in the community for this type of training. Pre-registration will be

required. If the need and interest is great enough, additional sessions will be offered. Statement of need Survey results clearly demonstrated the need for basic computer classes. Library staff distributed surveys at the library, elementary school, local businesses, staff, board members, and to city employees. Fifty-four surveys were returned and twenty-two indicated a desire for basic computer skill classes at the library. The library has also received several calls and face-to-face patron requests from adults to add basic computer classes. (Slonaker, 2013, p. 8)

Like many programming events, the success of digital literacy training sessions is dependent on the location where the training takes place, the topics that may bring broad community interest, and the training staff members who are capable and passionate about the sessions. Ferrari (2013) summarized a webinar organized from WebJunction.org with two rural library managers and suggested that a more ideal setting for training sessions is a classroom or meeting room with mobile computers rather than the library's public computers, since mobile computers can be used outside the library building, for example, reading in a senior center or in a one-to-one session. Library staff members with a desire to help people can learn of new technologies from volunteers or local colleges and, in return, train local residents. Libraries can also recruit trainers from local talent, such as senior volunteers, high school students, city information technology (IT) people, teachers, professional instructors, local businesses, and other educators in the community, as well as partner with other libraries, and so on. WebJunction also listed training handouts and topics that can be used by libraries here: http://www.webjunction.org/news/webjunction/teaching -technology-small-rural-libraries.html.

Librarians should collect evaluation data after training sessions to ensure the effectiveness of teaching. The purpose of the evaluation is not to survey user satisfaction, but to understand the effectiveness of the instruction and use the data to improve future evaluations. There are many freely available evaluation forms to use online. For example, Xie and Bugg (2009) also published their work regarding public library computer training for older adults seeking health information online. The ALA website also lists sample forms for library information literacy class evaluations (http://www.ala.org/offices /sites/ala.org.offices/files/content/ola/informationliteracy.pdf). In their book, Blake, Martin, and Du (2011) gave a sample evaluation form for a computer skills workshop (p. 75). All these resources can help librarians to evaluate and improve their literacy classes and training sessions.

CONCLUSION

New librarians need to adjust to their new social roles as educators in order to enhance community learning and to contribute to increasing the value to the neighborhood; librarians are the technology support and training staff for library stakeholders to attend digital literacy classes, as well as the hosts of the community common space where cultural and leisure activities take place.

Rural library directors may not have time to be trained during the transition period. They might find fellow librarians from other cities, as well as a library network nearby, which are both good resources to help them out when in the early stages of their career.

Rural libraries are expected to become community information anchors and support the community with free broadband Internet access and to enhance digital inclusion in rural communities. They are the backbones of digital literacy training to the general public, and they must recruit trainers and volunteers so that all community residents may become proficient users of information and communication technologies.

REFERENCES

Alemanne, N. D., Mandel, L. H., & McClure, C. R. (2011). The rural public library as leader in community broadband services. *Library Technology Reports, 47*(6), 19–28.

American Library Association. (n.d.). E-rate and universal service. Chicago, IL: American Library Association. Available at http://www.ala.org/advocacy/telecom/erate

Blake, M., Martin, R., & Du. Y. (2011). *Successful community outreach: A how-to-do it manual for librarians.* Chicago, IL: ALA Neal-Schuman.

Carmichael, L. R., McClure, C. R., Mandel, L. H., & Mardis, M. A. (2012). Practical approaches and proposed strategies for measuring selected aspects of community-based broadband deployment and use. *International Journal of Communication, 6*(2012), 2445–2466.

Chant, I. (2014). Gates Foundation prepares to exit library ecosystem. *Library Journal,* 139(11), p. 12. Available at http://lj.libraryjournal.com/2014/05/budgets-funding/gates -foundation-prepares-to-exit-library-ecosystem/#_

Connected Nation. (2011). Broadband readiness index. Washington, DC: Connected Nation. Available at http://www.connectednation.org/sites/default/files/broadband _readiness_index.pdf

Ferrari, A. (2013). *Teaching technology in small and rural libraries.* Seattle, WA: WebJunction. Available at http://www.webjunction.org/news/webjunction/teaching -technology-small-rural-libraries.html

Flatley, R., & Wyman, A. (2009). Changes in rural libraries and librarianship: A comparative survey. *Public Library Quarterly, 28*(1), 25–26.

Freeman, R. E., Harrison, J. S., Wicks, A. C., Parmar, B. L., & De Colie, S. (2010). *Stakeholder theory: The state of the art.* Cambridge, United Kingdom: Cambridge University Press.

Gorden, R. S. (2006). *The nextgen librarian's survival guide.* Medford, NJ: Information Today.

Harding, J. (2008). Information literacy and the public library: We've talked the talk, but are we walking the walk? *Australian Library Journal, 57*(3), 274–294.

Henderson, E. (2009). *Service trends in U.S. public libraries, 1997–2007.* Washington, DC: Institute of Museum and Library Services. Retrieved from http://www.imls .gov/pdf/Brief2010_01.pdf

Hoffman, J., Bertot, J. C., & Davis, D. M. (2012). Libraries connect communities: Public Library Funding & Technology Access Study 2011–2012 [Digital supplement]. *American Libraries.* Available at http://viewer.zmags.com/publication/4673a369

Institute of Museum and Library Services. (2012). *Building digital communities: Getting started.* Washington, DC: Institute of Museum and Library Services. Available at https://www.imls.gov/assets/1/AssetManager/BuildingDigitalCommunities _Framework.pdf

Jeager, P. T., McClure, C. R., & Bertot, J. C. (2005). The E-rate program and libraries and library consortia, 2000–2004: Trends and issues. *Information Technology and Libraries, 24*(2), 57–67.

Kruger, L. G., & Gilroy, A. A. (2013). *Broadband Internet access and the digital divide: Federal assistance programs* (Report number RL30719). Washington, DC: Congressional Research Service. Available at https://www.fas.org/sgp/crs/misc /RL30719.pdf

Mandel, L. H., Alemanne, N. D., & McClure, C. R. (2012). Rural anchor institution broadband connectivity: Enablers and barriers to adoption. In *Proceedings of the 2012 iConference* (pp. 136–144). New York: The Association for Computing Machinery. doi:10.1145/2132176.2132194

National broadband map. (2013). Available at http://www.broadbandmap.gov/technology

Real, B., Berto, J. C., & Jaeger, P. T. (2014). Rural public libraries and digital inclusion: Issues and challenges. *Information Technology and Libraries, 33*(1), 6–24.

Slonaker, M. (2013). *Chico Public Library, Inc. community outreach plan.* Denton, TX: PEARL Project, University of North Texas. Available at https://pearl.unt.edu /sites/default/files/chicopubliclibrarycommunityoutreachplan.pdf

Smith, A. (2010). *Home broadband 2010.* Washington, DC: Pew Research Center. Available at http://www.pewinternet.org/2010/08/11/home-broadband-2010/

Thibodeau, L. S. (2010). Networking Alaska public libraries [Data file]. Washington, DC: BroadbandUSA. Available at http://www2.ntia.doc.gov/files/grantees/alaskadeptofeed _pcc_application.pdf

United States Census Bureau. (2010). 2010 census urban and rural classification and urban area criteria [Data file]. Washington, DC: U.S. Census Bureau. Available at http://www.census.gov/geo/www/ua/2010urbanruralclass.html

United States Federal Communications Commission. (2015a). *Universal service program for schools and libraries (E-Rate).* Washington, DC: Federal Communications Commission. Available at: https://www.fcc.gov/general/universal-service -program-schools-and-libraries-e-rate

United States Federal Communications Commission. (2015b). *Connect America Fund (CAF).* Washington, DC: Federal Communications Commission. Available at https:// www.fcc.gov/general/connect-america-fund-caf

University of Minnesota Duluth. (2011). *Minnesota public libraries' return on investment.* Duluth, MN: University of Minnesota Duluth. Available at http://melsa.org /melsa/assets/File/Library_final.pdf

Xie, B., & Bugg, J. M. (2009). Public library computer training for older adults to access high-quality Internet health information. *Library & Information Science Research, 31*(3), 155–162.

CHAPTER FIVE

Nourishing Diversity

Diversity is a very established topic in library service and sometimes an ambiguous one. Multiple stages of diversity research have drawn different definitions. Winston (1999) recommended a number of factors to be considered in diversity research in LIS, which include the concept of diversity; the importance of the concept in a professional, interpersonal, and societal context; and the goals, objectives, and success involved in achieving diversity. Clara M. Chu, chair of the ALISE Diversity Statement Taskforce (2012), defined diversity as the representation of the wide variety of backgrounds (including racial, cultural, linguistic, gender, religious, international, socioeconomic, sexual orientation, differently abled, age among others) that people possess and that it is often used to address quantitative requirements/agendas/goals, whereas inclusion refers to what happens to people once they are in an organization, institution, or social context.

James O. Freeman from Dartmouth College stated: "The fundamental reason that diversity is important is that we are a diverse country, and our leadership is necessarily going to have to be drawn from a spectrum of ethnic, religious, and racial groups if we are to be successful as a democracy" (McLaughlin, 1991, p. 25).

Dakshinamurti (2006, p. 51) summarized three areas that are relevant to libraries: developing library collections that reflect the needs of diverse communities, providing services to diverse library patrons, and developing a diverse workforce in library settings. This chapter will discuss the overview of serving diverse users in libraries, including cultural, linguistic, socioeconomic, and age diversity, with less attention paid to racial, gender, religious, international, sexual orientation, and differently abled diversity. It will be followed by building multicultural collections, serving English as second language (ESL) and immigrant users, conducting outreach to diverse and multicultural communities, and promoting digital inclusion in rural communities and their diverse populations.

OVERVIEW OF DIVERSITY IN LIBRARY SERVICES

Libraries have the responsibility of respecting and preserving diverse traditions for their community users. This section discusses the status of diversity in library services followed by small libraries serving diverse linguistics users.

Status of Diversity in Library Services

Diversity refers in this book as different people who live in the United States, which may be one of the most culturally diverse countries in the world. The United States is a unique country with rich ethnic diversity within communities almost everywhere. With the exception of the Native American population, ancestors came from different parts of the globe. Some immigrants will stay in one place, but many will move to different places, including rural areas. For generations, various cultures and languages are more or less preserved in various communities in the United States, making linguistic diversity a focus when a population has new immigrants coming in larger groups. The influx of groups from Vietnam at the close of that war is one example. At the present time, communities with church sponsorship are accepting large numbers of immigrants from war torn countries such as the Sudan. Each year, the United States alone accepts 70,000 immigrants as refugees (http://www.immigrationpolicy.org/just-facts/refugees-fact-sheet).

Among the immigrants, Latinos are one of the fastest growing populations in the Unites States. Long (2011) defines Latinos as persons of Latin American origin rather than encompassing all Spanish-speaking people of the world. Ruhlman (2014) suggested that the Latino community is extremely diverse; some speak fluent English, some speak a little or none at all, and some speak indigenous languages. For immigrants, prior experience from native countries may influence their use of libraries. She commented that the language and literacy struggles also contribute toward word-of-mouth over written communication. She also commented that since the word "library" resembles "libreria," which means bookstore in Spanish, many Latinos think they cannot afford the library, or they will ask how much the books cost.

Traditionally Latinos are immigrants who like to keep their traditions and cultural identity and rely on others who speak their language and share the same immigration experience. Based on their research on Latinos in Arizona, Adkins, and Burns (2013) commented that while Latinos transition from their native language, for example Spanish or indigenous languages, to English in generations, the growth of the Latino population through immigration guarantees that the Spanish language is reinforced and retained in communities. Plocharezyk (2005) also commented that immigrant families who remain connected to their native language, customs, and values enable their children to nurture a strong self-esteem and identity as tools needed to combat over discrimination.

Small Libraries Nourishing Linguistic Diversity

The library as a community center is naturally a good candidate for diverse community users to network and celebrate the diverse language and cultural backgrounds of their community residents. The surveys conducted in 1999 and 2009 of public libraries in Arizona by the Adkins and Burns study (2013) found a huge increase in the percentage of libraries in Arizona offering services for Spanish-speakers in terms of Spanish-speaking librarians (47%), Spanish-speaking clerks (62%), Spanish-language adult books (93%), children's books (100%), and music recordings (79%), but there is still not enough of an increase of quantities compared with the increase of services to Latinos.

While most new immigrants are likely to initially stay in large cities such as New York, Los Angeles, Chicago, Miami, Houston, and other metropolitan areas, more and more small and rural towns are seeing an influx of new immigrants. This changes local communities. For example, immigrants may not be citizens, which means they cannot vote. "Many cities and towns are thick with residents who cannot vote, run for office, sit on juries, and otherwise hold governments accountable" (Rinaldi, 2014). Small towns also need to cope with linguistic diversity as new immigrants move in. As Mertens (2015) reported:

> For two decades, rural communities across the Midwest have been finding ways to absorb Latino immigrants. Now, a new generation of immigrants arriving from far-flung places such as Myanmar, Somalia, Iraq, and West Africa has brought a bewildering variety of cultures and languages.

Building multicultural environments will likely attract and retain new businesses and new populations, two of the main reasons a rural community loses tax revenue as a source of income.

Music and art festivals are a great way to blend immigration culture with local culture. Such activities likely cannot be organized by libraries alone but can be held via partnerships with local municipal governments, parks and recreation centers, Rotary clubs, and literacy organizations. Many libraries have participated in local festivals and events, making sure that the libraries have a presence in such community events.

When librarians are allied with diverse populations, their libraries can regularly host successful cultural programs and attract local user groups. This may build strong support for the library in difficult times.

Small Libraries Nourishing Socioeconomic Diversity

Socioeconomic status is one major indicator of diversity that shapes rural and small library services. Socioeconomic status is defined by the U. S. National Center for Education Statistics (2012) as "one's access to financial, social, cultural, and human capital resources," and traditionally it includes income levels, education, and occupational status, with additional measures such as household, neighborhood, and school resources (p. 4). Socioeconomic diversity influences many areas of library services, including the educational preparedness level of children, community economic well-being, and local support for libraries and schools (Johnson, Showalter, Klein, & Lester, 2014).

The same report by Johnson et al. (2014) found that rural residents in 11 states in Central Appalachia, the Southeast, and the Mid-south Delta have the lowest high school graduation rate, under 81%. Parental educational, one factor of social economic status, may influence the child's reading literacy level. One of the busiest time for rural and small libraries is summer, when libraries provide summer reading programs that allow children from diverse background to increase their literacy skills, which in the long run improve their academic potential.

People with lower levels of education tend to have less training and job security. Many rural areas pay less and have higher unemployment rates. In contrast, small towns near a large urban area may have more affluent residents commute to work, more families move in, or an influx of retired residents. The difference in income levels, education, and job status can create diverse information needs in a community. Bernard Vavrek, the founder of the Association for Rural & Small Libraries, called this phenomenon "exodus to rural areas" which brought additional challenges to rural library services (Vavrek, 1995a, p. 24).

Small Libraries Nourishing Age Diversity

As mentioned in Chapter 1, children, young people, and old people have different reading habits, Internet usage, and technology proficiency. Public libraries serve "from cradle to grave" (http://www.ala.org/educationcareers /careers/librarycareerssite/typesoflibraries). Unlike bigger libraries, where there are different departments of service, such as youth, teens, and adults, rural and small libraries with limited staff must serve all age groups. For example, Jacobs (2013, p. 336) observed that those library users who need technical assistance and help with information literacy training, are the elderly, the less-educated, the poor, and the members of minority groups. Public Broadcasting Service (2014) reported that cost and technology skills still limit many seniors from going online, but those who were helped to use computers for online communications "feel like there's a sense of freedom and opportunity in that process" and "are able to use e-mail, and all of a sudden they're actually communicating with a friend or a loved one far away." On the contrary, younger generations use computers and mobile devices as naturally as pens and pencils, which makes it meaningful to promote library programs that bring different age groups together.

Intergenerational programs bring children, youth, and older adults together: grandparents and grandchildren reading programs, family literacy, art, board games, computer classes, and so on. An example of this is the Allegheny County Library Association in Pennsylvania, which promotes intergenerational library programs and presents biannual awards to participating libraries. Among them are "Adopt a Grandparent Storytimes," "Wii Bowling Tournaments," and "Grandmorning" (http://www.aclalibraries.org/general /the_intergenerational_library.html). Both rural and small town libraries can benefit from such programs that bring diverse age groups of users together. One of the most likely services that can be offered to potential library clients is a collection that serves their needs. The next section discusses building multicultural and multilingual collections.

MULTICULTURAL AND MULTILINGUAL COLLECTIONS

The ALA RUSA Guidelines encourages libraries to provide an effective, balanced, and substantial collection for each ethnic, cultural, and linguistic groups (Reference and User Services Association, 2007). This section will first address the philosophy of building multicultural collections.

Philosophy of Building Multicultural Collections

Libraries should provide an equitable level of service to all members of their communities regardless of ethnic, cultural, or linguistic background (Reference and User Services Association, 2007). Public librarians can benefit from fostering an intercultural dialog and reaching out to all members of the local community, especially multicultural populations (Tanackovic, Lacovic, & Stanarevic, 2012). The philosophy of cultural diversity in library services finds its roots in the commitment of human rights and freedom, including people of different ethnic, linguistic, and cultural backgrounds (United Nations, 1948). Article 27 of Human Rights Declaration states:

1. Everyone has the right freely to participate in the cultural life of the community, to enjoy the arts and to share in scientific advancement and its benefits.
2. Everyone has the right to the protection of the moral and material interests resulting from any scientific, literary or artistic production of which he is the author (p. 7).

English language learners, or ELL, refers to those people in the community who are new to the country and speak multiple languages. There is a tremendous practical interest in serving this group of residents in recent years, particularly in response to the infusion of new immigrants from many different countries who bring various talents into the workforce from different cultural backgrounds.

Multicultural library collections may create a sense of belonging in their new communities for these new immigrants. Moreover, materials in their native languages help patrons by offering lifelong learning for people for whom English is a second language. Diverse collections will help all community users to accept differences and increase their knowledge of the world.

Guidelines of Building Multilingual Collections

As cited in previous sections, the American Library Association division Reference and User Service Association (2007) published its guidelines for libraries building multilingual collections. It states, "Providing library materials for ethnic, cultural and linguistic groups should not be seen as an 'additional' or 'extra' service, but as an integral part of every library's services. Libraries should establish goals, objectives, and policies that integrate multilingual services into their overall work plan."

A Canadian study by Dilevko and Dali (2002) found that budgetary restriction leads to libraries only building multilingual collections where there are enough funds or donations from the community. They suggested building such collections according to user needs analysis and sometimes even building proportionally more collections in a language in order to establish minimally effective collections (http://www.moyak.com/papers/multilingual-library-collections.html). In this way the library's multicultural collection is likely to be effective in its use, and the collection will start attracting multilingual users to the library.

Libraries can build various collections for its multicultural community. One kind of such a collection can provide immigration and naturalization resources so immigrants can move from being undocumented immigrants to becoming citizens. Libraries can provide authentic and free resources to help immigrants with their personal immigration journey without needing to hire lawyers at every step. One such resource is the U.S. Citizenship and Immigration Services, which has provided a toolkit to train the immigrants' communities on job seeking, health care, business, and so on. (http://www.uscis.gov/sites/default/files/USCIS/files/Toolkit_Quick_Start_Guide.pdf).

ESL AND IMMIGRANT USERS IN LIBRARIES

Linguistic diversity is a challenge for immigrants who have a wide range of skills and educational backgrounds. In order to be employed in the new country, they often are required have literacy skills in the English language. It is not uncommon to see highly educated immigrants applying for low-skilled, low-paying jobs in various professions. They have different needs concerning literacy and cultural integration. American public libraries have a tradition of serving users from different cultures, including foreign-born residents. Providing literacy instruction for all residents is one of those services. This may be expanded to offer ESL classes or to help patrons locate them. Burke (2008) commented that in recent years most immigrants were from Latin America and Asia. She concluded that there are several areas that public libraries can improve on in order to serve immigrant users. Regarding collections and programs, libraries should build current collections of materials in the immigrants' language and topics of interests, as well as programs on immigration law, citizenship, job searching, health care, and literacy; some ideas for doing this may be in the U.S. Immigration Toolkit. Regarding library staff recruitment and training, she suggested hiring bilingual staff or volunteers and training library staff to be respectful to immigrants' culture. Libraries should also be in touch with the immigrants' community and promote the library to community centers, community leaders, social service centers, and schools, as well as bookmobiles, branches, and so on (Burke, 2008, p. 166). Cuban (2008) summarized successful literacy programs that a library can adopt: for example, facilitating conversation groups, enhancing leaner leadership on public speaking and collaboration, promoting health literacy projects, organizing storytelling in a celebration of learning, providing civic education and citizenship, and developing users' bilingual and native language literacy.

However, the information use and seeking behaviors of immigrants are different from those who are born and raised in the United States. Immigrant library users may feel out of touch with the new culture, and they may have the need for belonging to the community. Library services to immigrants make them feel welcomed, and even "like family" (Cuban, 2008, p. 6). Otherwise, immigrants could be intimidated by library buildings and staff. Long (2011) cited the book by Luevano-Molina (2001) with a survey of immigrant Mexican residents in Southern California who are "insecure towards public library staff" and "deliberately choose to patronize libraries in which they feel culturally validated." (p. 505)

OUTREACH TO SOCIOECONOMIC AND AGE DIVERSITY

Library services to multicultural communities include developing collections, services, and programs that promote inclusion. Libraries see the need to reach out to multicultural communities especially in the area of Internet use. Very much has changed since 2007, when only 56% of Latinos, or 14% of the U.S. population, went online; today education and English proficiency are still good predictors of whether to go online or not. For example, Internet use is uniformly low for whites (32%), Hispanics (31%), and African Americans (25%) who have not completed high school (Fox & Livingston, 2007). Brown and Lopez (2015) believe immigrant Hispanics pose both a challenge and an opportunity to the library community. Half of them have never visited a U.S. public library, but Hispanic immigrants who use public libraries stand out as the most appreciative of what libraries can offer, from free books to research resources to the fact that libraries tend to offer a quiet, safe space. They are the very outspoken supporters when a library faces budget cuts or even closing.

To achieve the goal of outreach to minority communities, libraries make an effort to understand the needs of the users from a multicultural perspective. One example is a parent and family digital literacy project with Latina/o immigrant parents in San Antonio, Texas (Machado-Casas, Sanchez, & Ed, 2014). This collaborative project includes a university teacher's academy with an elementary school and the surrounding community and families. Most families were Mexican nationals or Mexican Americans, with one or two children enrolled in the school taught by student teachers. During the workshop, families worked on a series of technology activities ranging from the most basic (turning the computer on) to creating a PowerPoint presentation or iMovie videos. Family participants help each other on learning, sharing, and teaching. They found Latino immigrants are family-oriented and ready to create emotive digital stories and learn to use technologies as a medium for expressing and building their parent-child bond. This research report suggests the need for librarians in rural communities to assess the technology needs particularly in the area of Internet usage. If patrons do not have Internet access at home, will they come to the library to learn how to access the Internet, and do they have the ability with the English language to do so?

DIVERSITY AND DIGITAL INCLUSION

Diversity has a new meaning today. Rural and small libraries need to include users who are not using digital resources and who have been excluded from the information society. This section introduces concepts of digital inclusion, social inclusion, and subjective norm. We will start with digital inclusion.

Digital Inclusion as a New Facet of Diversity

There is a well-documented discussion on the social division that exists between those who have information resources and those who do not (Walker & Walker, 1997). The relevant concepts include information inequalities, digital divide, information poverty, and recently, social exclusion from the information society. Rather than focus on gaps of information access, the concept of digital inclusion focuses on activities that narrow the digital divide and enhance digital literacy. Digital inclusion refers to any strategies that provide training, services, or opportunities designed to address the challenges of the digitally disadvantaged (Jaeger, Bertot, Thompson, Katz, & Decoster, 2012).

Under the umbrella of diversity, digital inclusion is part of the effort to promote social inclusion. Social exclusion was considered the dynamic process of being shut out, fully or partially, from any of the social, economic, political, or cultural systems that determine the social integration of a person in society (Yu, 2006). Munck (2005) suggested that social inclusion be multidimensional and multidisciplinary in the way it approaches social inequality.

Vavrek (1995b) concluded that rural and small towns are traditionally conservative, and their library trustees or board members see no reason to change the routine of life in their favorite place. Atkinson and Marlier (n.d.) suggested that new knowledge should be selectively introduced into the information world of disadvantaged people. A condition that influences this process is the relevance of that information in response to everyday problems and concerns.

Social Inclusion and Subjective Norm

It seems a natural step to enhance the social inclusion of rural libraries by introducing community outreach plans and partnership opportunities. This involves the subjective norm, which is "the perceived social pressure to perform or not to perform the behavior" in question (Ajzen, 1991, p. 188). This concept is developed from a previous theory of reasoned action on "a person's belief that specific individuals or groups think he/she should or should not perform a behavior and his/her motivation to comply with the specific referents" (Ajzen & Fishbein, 1980, p. 8). It is a similar term, but it is used in different behavior models, with the formal model more focused on attitude toward intention, while the latter model is more focused on intention to actual behavior.

In essence, if the community's social pressure encourages diversity, then individuals will think it is normal to engage in culturally diverse events. Subjective norms as represented by normative beliefs are located within the broader construct of social norms. "While a social norm is usually meant to refer to a rather broad range of permissible, but not necessarily required behaviors, NB (Normative Belief) refers to a specific behavioral act as the performance of which is expected or desired under the given circumstances" (Ajzen & Fishbein, 1972, p. 2). Ajzen and Fishbein (1980) suggested a person's intention to a certain behavior is determined by three things: a person's attitude toward a specific behavior, his or her subjective norms, and his or her perceived behavioral control. Intention is believed to be a good indicator of action but does not necessarily lead to real action. To influence the rural librarians' intention for social engagement and innovation, it is necessary to change their attitude and intention toward such innovation. Another way is to create virtual communities and to make it easier to join the critical mass. Subjective norm may provide a certain degree of support needed in order to change community residents' behavior, and become more tolerant of the library's efforts to engage diverse populations and include the socially underserved populations in library programs.

To nourish cultural diversity and promote social inclusion, it seems natural to use the tools we discussed in previous chapters such as community outreach and partnership opportunities in rural library settings. Such community outreach plans may provide a plan of action and strategic approach for the librarian and can be a useful tool to strengthen already effective ongoing relationships and gain support from local governing agencies, civic organizations, community service organizations, and leaders in the community.

While the chapter has not had a focus on racial, gender, religious, international, sexual orientation, and differently abled characteristics, these areas of diversity may be researched in the following resources listed in the appendix. Please do research their needs when you have patrons who are in those diverse categories.

CONCLUSION

In the past, diversity was used to describe race, gender, or ethnicity, regardless of country of origin, income level, socioeconomic status, or age. The definition of diversity is changing rapidly in the digital era. The U.S. immigration status and demographic changes indicate that previous terms, such as "minorities," have new meanings today; in some parts of the communities in the country, Latinos or even Asians are the majority in the cities.

Libraries, no matter their size, need to be aware of any non-English speaking segments of their community in order to promote English as a second language and develop multicultural and multilingual collections. Immigrants need to feel at home in libraries, enjoy diverse collections on their own culture, and have the opportunity to take literacy and language classes in order to prepare to contribute to the workforce and to eventually perform civic duties.

Library leaders must be aware of socioeconomic diversity in their community in order to respond to the needs of this group by providing information relevant to their economic situation, and by providing access to technology. Programs teaching these users how to use the Internet, develop computer skills, and understand social media are especially beneficial. Library service to diverse users should also consider older people living in rural and remote areas, who might be older and have less mobility to access a library in their communities.

Digital inclusion helps to create virtual communities. Libraries should pay attention to promoting digital inclusion by expending their services through outreach to target groups. This will enable the library to attract funders and sponsors, as well as better serve its community.

REFERENCES

Adkins, D., & Burns, C. S. (2013). Arizona public libraries serving Spanish-speaking: Context for changes. *Reference & User Services Quarterly, 53*(1), 60–69.

Ajzen, I. (1991). The theory of planned behavior. *Organizational Behavior and Human Decision Processes, 50,* 179–211.

Ajzen, I., & Fishbein, M. (1972). Attitudes and normative beliefs as factors influencing behavioral intentions. *Journal of Personality and Social Psychology, 21*(1), 1–9.

Ajzen, I., & Fishbein, M. (1980). *Understanding attitudes and predicting social behavior.* Englewood Cliffs, NJ: Prentice-Hall.

ALISE Diversity Task Force. (2012). ALISE Diversity Statement. Available at http://www.alise.org/alise---alise-diversity-statement

Atkinson, A. B., & Marlier, E. (2010). *Analysing and measuring social inclusion in a global context.* New York: United Nations Publication. Available at http://www.un.org/esa/socdev/publications/measuring-social-inclusion.pdf

Brown, A., & Lopez, M. H. (2015). *Public libraries and Hispanics.* Washington, DC: Pew Research Center. Available at http://www.pewhispanic.org/2015/03/17/public-libraries-and-hispanics/

Burke, S. (2008). Use of public libraries by immigrants. *Reference & User Services Quarterly, 48*(2), 164–174.

Casas, M., Sanchez, P., & Ek, L. (2014). The digital literacy practices of Latina/o immigrant parents in an after-school technology partnership. *Multicultural Education, 21*(3/4), 28–33.

Cuban, S. (2008). *Serving new immigrant communities in the library.* Westport, CT: Libraries Unlimited.

Dakshinamurti, G. B. (2006). Diversity in libraries: A Canadian perspective. In B. I. Dewey & L. Parham (Eds.), *Achieving diversity: A how-to-do manual for libraries* (pp. 51–57). New York: Neal-Schumann.

Dilevko, J., & Dali, K. (2002). The challenge of building multilingual collections in Canadian public libraries. *Library Resources & Technical Services, 46*(4), 116–137.

Fox, S., & Livingston, G. (2007). *Latinos online: Hispanics with lower levels of education and English proficiency remain largely disconnected from the Internet.* Washington, DC: The Pew Hispanic Center. Available at http://www.pewhispanic.org/files/reports/73.pdf

Jacobs, M. (2013). *Electronic resources librarianship and management of digital information.* New York: Routledge

Jaeger, P. T., Bertot, J. C., Thompson, K. M., Katz, S. M., & Decoster, E. J. (2012). The intersection of public policy and public access: Digital divides, digital literacy, digital inclusion, and public libraries. *Public Library Quarterly, 31*(1), 1–20.

Johnson, J., Showalter, D., Klein, R., & Lester, C. (2014). *Why rural matters 2013–2014: The condition of rural education in the 50 states.* Washington, DC: Rural School and Community Trust. Available at http://www.ruraledu.org/user_uploads/file/2013-14-Why-Rural-Matters.pdf

Long, D. (2011). Latino students' perceptions of the academic library. *The Journal of Academic Librarianship, 37*(6), 504–511.

Luevano-Molina, S. (2001). Mexican/Latino immigrants and the Santa Ana Libraries: An urban ethnography. In S. Lúevano-Molina (Ed.), *Immigrant politics and the public library.* Westport, CT: Greenwood.

Madanipour, A., Cars, G., & Allen, J. (1998). *Social exclusion in European cities: Processes, experiences and responses.* London, United Kingdom: Jessica Kingsley.

McLaughlin, J. B. (1991). James O. Freeman on diversity & Dartmouth. *Change, 23*(September/October), 25–31.

Mertens, R. (2015). For small-town America, new immigrants pose linguistic, cultural challenges. *Christian Science Monitor.* Available at http://www.csmonitor.com/USA/Society/2015/0314/For-small-town-America-new-immigrants-pose-linguistic-cultural-challenges

Munck, R. (2005). *Globalization and social exclusion: A transformationalist perspective.* Bloomfield, CT: Kumarian Press.

National Center for Education Statistics. (2012). Improving the measurement of socioeconomic status for the national assessment of educational progress: A theoretical foundation. Available at http://nces.ed.gov/nationsreportcard/pdf/researchcenter/Socioeconomic_Factors.pdf

Plocharezyk, L. (2005). Meeting multicultural needs in school libraries: An examination of Mexican migrant families and factors that influence academic success. *Journal of Access Services, 3*(4), 45–50.

Public Broadcasting Service. (2014). Closing the digital divide by helping seniors get online. Available at http://www.pbs.org/newshour/bb/nation-jan-june14-seniors-01-13/

Reference and User Services Association. (2007). Guidelines for the development and promotion of multilingual collections and services. Chicago, IL: American Library Association. Available at http://www.ala.org/rusa/resources/guidelines /guidemultilingual

Rinaldi, M. (2014). *Immigration puts small town on cultural divide*. Boston, MA: Boston Globe. Available at https://www.bostonglobe.com/news/nation/2014/01/05 /small-town-immigration-creates-great-cultural-divide/7rtIuuAo8fj85MdeniW52M /story.html

Ruhlman, E. (2014). Connecting Latinos with libraries. *American Libraries, 45*(5), 36–40.

Tanackovic, S. F., Lacovic, D., & Stanarevic. (2012). Public libraries and linguistic diversity: A Small scale study on the Slovak ethnic minority in eastern Croatia. *Libri, 62*(1), 52–66.

United Nations. (1948). *Universal declaration of human rights*. New York: United Nations. Available at http://www.un.org/en/documents/udhr/

Vavrek, B. (1995a). Rural information needs and the role of the public library. *Library Trends, 44*(1), 21–48.

Vavrek, B. (1995b). Rural libraries and community development. *Wilson Library Bulletin, 69*, 42–44.

Walker, A., & Walker, C. (1997). *Britain divided: The growth of social exclusion in the 1980s and 1990s*. London, United Kingdom: Child Poverty Action Group.

Winston, M. (1999). Introduction. In M. Winston (Ed.), *Managing multiculturalism and diversity in the library: Principles and issues for administrators* (pp. 1–3). Philadelphia, PA: Haworth Press.

Yu, L. (2006). Understanding information inequality: Making sense of the literature of the information and digital divides. *Journal of Library and Information Science, 38*(4), 229–252. doi:10.1177/096100060607060

CHAPTER SIX

Fostering Collaboration and Entrepreneurship

Libraries are sensitive to local political and funding changes. Stenström and Haycock (2014) emphasized the importance of research on libraries in the political context. A common misunderstanding is that the increased library use will result in the increased attention of library stakeholders such as city managers. However, increased library use does not correlate to increased funding, because user groups alone cannot influence the annual budgetary process in public libraries. External pressure to a library's funding unit, for example, local political and partisan initiatives, the image of a city, the credibility of the unit where a library reports, and perception of libraries, play more important roles.

At the same time, librarians need to seek all funding opportunities using various library programs and community events to make them fundraising opportunities. The social networking tools in the digital era may provide opportunities for libraries to raise funds using limited budgets, time, and effort. This is more easily accomplished if collaboration is sought between partners in the community. This chapter discusses funding public libraries, sources of funds, seeking partners in fundraising efforts, writing grants, and social networking. Finally, the library is described as a nonprofit business.

FUNDING IN PUBLIC LIBRARIES

Nationwide, only 1% of the operating revenue of public libraries is directly or indirectly from federal sources, with 10% from state sources, and the majority of the funding, 82%, is from local government sources. The remaining 8% comes from monetary gifts and donations, grants, interest, library fines, and fees for library services (Owens & Sieminski, 2007). A 2013 Institute of Museum and Library Services (IMLS) report confirmed little changes on the distribution, as 84.8% of the revenue continues to come from local sources (Swan et al., 2013, p. 19).

History of Federal Funding in Public Libraries

Farrell (2012) reviewed the history of federal support to libraries in the United States and suggested that one of the first governmental library programs was the result of the establishment of the Printing Act of 1895, stemming from the Government Printing Office submission of documents to the federal depositories. This was designed to ensure a cost-effective and efficient way to access many government publications. The 19th century was the time when each state began to build its own legislative libraries, and by the end of the century all states had a state library in their capitol.

After World War II, regional libraries were developed in many places in the country. The 1956 Library Services Act authorized federal support to library services for working and low-income people as well as rural areas with populations of less than 10,000. In 1960 the law was extended to authorize 7.5 million dollars in federal funding to urban areas as well as the rest of rural areas in the country. In 1963, President Kennedy recommended amending the Library Services Act (LSA) to fund urban and rural libraries for construction as well as operation, and the U.S. Congress passed the Library Services and Construction Act (LSCA) in 1964, signed into law by President Johnson. The LSA and LSCA have provided federal funding to libraries for decades, and the level of library services to the American public was improved considerably (Fry, 1975).

As early as the 1980s, many librarians felt that some of the original goals of the LSCA had been accomplished and that federal funds could be used to meet new needs such as digital technologies and electronic resources. The Library Services and Technology Act (LSTA) of 1996 continued to support the rural and underserved populations and expanded all federal funding support from public libraries to all types of libraries; this act included the creation of IMLS, the primary source of federal support for the nation, consisting of 123,000 libraries and 35,000 museums (imls.gov). IMLS provides funding to state and local libraries, museums, and library education programs. Gregory (1999, p. 378) stated:

> With passage of LSTA, responsibility for library services was moved from the Department of Education to the newly created Institute of Museum and Library Services (IMLS), an independent federal agency that is part of the National Foundation on the Arts and Humanities. As a smaller independent agency, the IMLS focuses on library programs in a way that the Department of Education did not.

Historically federal funding, mainly channeled through state library agencies, has provided local library access to electronic databases and subscriptions to digital materials, for example, TexShare Databases in Texas, the Power Library in Pennsylvania, the FIND-IT! ILLINOIS in Illinois, and the Ohio WebLibrary in Ohio, among others (https://www.dallas.edu/library /Statewide%20Library%20Resources%20by%20State.pdf). However, small rural libraries may not have trained staff or the equipment or access to use these opportunities. Some regulations require a library to be accredited by the state, and if a small community library does not generate enough operating funds to meet the minimum accreditation standards, it is often not qualified to use the state-level databases. Such libraries will in return get less support from federal and state levels.

Local Government Funding

State and Local Government Funding

The majority of the funding for public libraries is from local venues, particularly local property tax or sales tax, but there is rarely a regulation dictating how much the city or country should fund a public library. Since local government funding is the main income of many public libraries, the city managers or local tax code will determine the portion of revenue distributed to the libraries. For small and rural libraries, the tax-based income may barely support the utilities and one part-time or full-time staff salary, with little left to support additional staff, materials, and any unexpected spending.

Local stakeholders such as mayors, city managers, or judges may to some degree control the distribution of the budget, but the willingness to support local public libraries is also determined by the general public, the voters, who ultimately decide the source of the local revenues and their distribution. Libraries are educational entities that support literacy for the local workforce, support the lifelong learning of local residents, and in the long run ensure a democratic society system. However, even when the mission and practice of public libraries are centered on the needs of the local public, with good communication of the library's mission, goals, and objectives to the public, a stable library support is still not necessarily a priority for the government officials funding libraries or the community, who often do not support bond issues to fund public libraries. It is definitely a part of the political process for the library director.

Sources of Nongovernment Funding

Merrifield (1995, p. 60) warned that "given the fact that the majority of public libraries in the United States rely on local funding for the bulk of their operating income, it is no wonder that most libraries continue to focus their efforts on increasing local funding." Overall, a rural library's funding support is diversified, not relying on federal or state support alone. Other revenues include local, regional, or multijurisdictional sources, including private sources such as foundations, friends groups, and corporations, or revenue generated by fines and fees for services (Institute of Museum and Library Services, 2010, p. 84).

Private Sources of Funding

Alternative funding sources range from local donations from friends of libraries, individuals, and groups to funds from corporate entities. The success of funding libraries through private sources varies. Libraries that cultivated attention and interest from generous donors have greater chances of receiving gifts and endowments in big sums that can often be used to fulfill major one-time projects such as a new building structure, utilities improvement, equipment purchases, and so on. Private donations can hardly be the sustainable main source of income for daily operations when no other venues of revenues are available. There are lots of successful cases of libraries raising consistent funds and endowments from local communities, and many of them are in the business sector.

Business Income

Librarians are very creative in securing income under this category. Space rental is one of the simpler methods of generating extra revenue for a library, with extra space if the market and local regulations allow, since some libraries are running as nonprofit businesses. One of the common sources of income is to have a bookstore, which is often managed by volunteers from the friends of libraries; for example, Alpine Public Library has a Re-reads Bookstore inside the main library that sells used books weeded from collections or donated books and DVDs from community users (http://alpinepubliclibrary.org/re-reads-bookstore/). Another way of gaining income is to rent part of library space for businesses or coffee shops. The American Library Association (ALA) hosted an unofficial Wiki page on bibliographies and names of libraries with coffee shops (http://wikis.ala.org/professionaltips/index.php?title=Libraries_with_Coffee_Shops). The national survey by the Pennsylvania Library Association (PaLA) and the Pennsylvania Citizens for Better Libraries (PCBL) reported survey results showing that among the 96 libraries that participated in their survey, 22 libraries reported having bookstores, 34 have rental space, and 19 have coffee shops (Owens & Sieminski, 2007, p. 74).

While overdue fines are a common supplementary income for libraries, some studies show the negative impact of library fines to users' behavior. West Virginia's Southern Area Public Library (SAPL), winner of the 2013 Best Small Libraries in America by *Library Journal* magazine, had a policy of not charging overdue fines but put a jar on the circulation desk with a sign suggesting that users contribute. They got more in donations than they would from fines and generated good feelings from patrons. Many libraries have creative ways to raise in-kind donations of goods, such as listing the needed books, CD, and DVD titles for donors, so donors can select and buy what the library needs.

GRANTS SOURCES AND GRANT AGENCIES

Grants sources include private individuals and foundations, as well as local, state, and federal government. There are also businesses and other agencies, such as nonprofits, which are sources for funding for libraries.

Grant Sources

Grants can be from federal, state, county, city, and municipal funding sources. Womack (2012) cautioned against writing grants as a process of simply filling out an application and submitting to the grant agency, but rather it should be a research skill that needs to be practiced. Proposals to private foundations can be short and focus on the problems and proposed solution, while federal competitive grants can be a lengthy research plan with detailed supporting documents. Grants provided by federal and state entities are often competitive in nature, which requires that the grant writers understand the mission, goals, and expectations of the grant agency and the scope of the grant. It is ideal to meet both the goals of the grant agency and the local needs and show how the proposed project will benefit the target audience of the project. Finally, it is often expected that the library staff is the grant writer and not a professional grant writer, as not only is it easier to write the grant with the target audience in mind but also it is more likely that the grant will be completed after it is awarded. For new rural and small librarians, it might be helpful to start with local and private foundations and then move to more competitive state and federal grants, possibly in collaboration with other libraries or agencies.

Several classic textbooks are available to help librarians in rural and small libraries pursue grants as well as funding support, such as the works by Dowlin (2008), Hall (2009), Herring (2004), Mackellar and Gerding (2010), and O'Neal-McElrath (2013). The more recent collection of papers on library best practices was compiled by Wood (2014). The ALA website has a link to the annotated bibliography on general and library-specific how-to manuals for grants and fundraising techniques, articles, and information for consultants (American Library Association, 2006). The resource is a little out of date today, but much of the information can still be useful in funding opportunities today.

Grant Agencies

Time after time, librarians in small and rural libraries find that grants are major necessities if they are going to update their collections, renovate furniture, and update the facilities. Sullivan (2007) listed three information sources for seeking grant funding for libraries: government, private, and additional sources, which include websites and publications. Government funding includes IMLS, mentioned earlier in the chapter. IMLS supports library programs such as the Laura Bush 21st Century Librarian Program,

National Leadership Grants for Libraries, and Native American Library Services grants for basic and enhanced services, as well as Native Hawaii Library Services.

Private foundations can be another important funding source for rural libraries. Librarians in rural and small libraries may have a list of local community foundations that have a track record of supporting these libraries. These foundations usually fund specific types of project proposals. They are often very local, for example, the McFeely-Rogers Foundation in Pennsylvania provides funding support to local educational and charitable associations in Latrobe, Pennsylvania. There are some that accept grant proposals from the state level. For example, the Tocker Foundation in Texas accepts library grants twice a year and sponsors rural and small librarians' travel to the Texas Library Association annual conference (http://www.tocker.org/). Scholastic.com lists dozens of foundations and ongoing-grant awards (http://www.scholastic.com /librarians/programs/grants.htm). Many of them provide books, audio/video materials, funding support for literacy projects, and travel grants to conferences. The foundations listed include the Starbucks Foundation (http://www .starbucks.com/responsibility/community/starbucks-foundation), the Libri Foundation (http://www.librifoundation.org/#GUIDE), and the W. K. Kellogg Foundation (http://www.wkkf.org/).

SEEKING PARTNERSHIP IN COMMUNITIES

Libraries Partner with Other Local Agencies

Why is partnership necessary for public libraries? Susan Benton, president of Urban Library Council, suggested that the value of public libraries is in achieving local sustainability. No matter how developed a community is, it is exposed to the vulnerability of the economy, environment, and population. With other local agencies, public libraries are natural partners to assist in the improvement of local economic development, environmental conservation, and equitable access to information for its citizens, for example, e-government projects, where "many public libraries have begun to collaborate with local government agencies and community organizations to provide vital services to their communities" (Bertot, Jaeger, Gorham, Taylor, & Lincoln, 2013, p. 127). Often businesses think the library is supported by the local government to which they pay taxes, and they are reluctant to be a part of funding ongoing expenses but are agreeable to funding a special project now and then. Public libraries make attractive partners for local businesses and government agencies focused on rural sustainability, since libraries do the following:

- Engage young children and their parents in reading and early literacy programs
- Provide social equity in terms of public access computers for local residents to improve computer literacy skills and apply for jobs online

• Assist in efforts and the local policy of energy preservation and the enhancement of natural resources and assets (Benton, 2010, p. 2)

Edwards, Rauseo, and Unger (2013) commented that "the combination of a shrinking budget for library staff and collection, and the onslaught of a technology mediated life, make the library more important in cultural and community life." Because libraries add value to the community by serving as cultural centers and because they are used by most residents, libraries deserve to be funded by local government and business.

Libraries need to reach out to local business and government leaders to support sustainability action plans, demonstrating how the library's early child development and literacy programs and technologies can help achieve local government priorities. In this way the library can supply success stories on supporting economic vitality, preserving natural resources, and supporting social equity and can be an advocate for the cities and counties that the library serves.

Factors of Successful Partnership

The *Public Library Quarterly* (2009) journal published an abridged version of the federal document on library services to immigrants, and the journal summarizes the essence of successful partnerships in a local context. Partnerships with organizations that serve immigrants "helps to leverage resources, provides avenues for sharing information at their events," provides speakers for events at the library, advises on effective ways to reach target audience members, [pay for handouts] and refers their immigrant clients to the library (p. 121).

Most western management philosophy emphasizes individual efforts and the standardization of work, such as those who work in assembly lines, but not the challenges of collaborative work (Giesecke, 2012). Recent work in the library and information science (LIS) field emphasized the merit of collaboration and partnership. In her work on school librarianship, theorist Montiel-Overall (2005) suggests that collaboration include efforts such as partnerships, interaction among coequals, information sharing and shared vision, joint negotiation of common ground, shared power, joint planning, complementary skills, strategic alliances, new value creation, and multiorganization processes (p. 3).

Kanter's Eight Is

Kanter (1994) concluded that there are Eight Is that create successful organizational relationships: individual excellence (both partners are strong and have something of value to contribute to the relationship), importance (the relationship fits major strategic objectives of the partners), interdependence (the partners need each other. Neither can accomplish alone what both can together), investment (the partners invest in each other), information (communication is reasonably open), integration (the partners develop linkages and shared ways of operation), institutionalization (the relationship is given a formal status, with clear responsibilities and decision processes), and integrity (the partners behave toward each other in honorable ways that justify and enhance mutual trust).

Gallop Partnership Rating Scale

Gallop Corporation created a toolkit to identify factors that enhance partnerships (Wagner & Muller, 2009). The Gallop Partnership Rating Scale is an instrument with 21 questions in 7 subscales that outline the factors that make for successful partnership. These 7 factors define successful partnerships. First, partners must have a *common mission*, a common purpose, and common goals. They need to ensure *fairness* and divide the workload fairly between partners. The next major factor is *trust*, since there is no genuine partnership without trust. The fourth factor is *acceptance*. Partners recognize and build on each other's strengths rather than concentrating on weaknesses. They accept each other for who they are rather than trying to change each other. *Forgiveness* is also necessary for a sustainable partnership. When mistakes or conflicts happen, partners need to forgive each other and rebuild the trust. Partners need to have good listening skills and also need good *communication* with each other, in order to share their expertise to solve problems. Finally, partnerships need the element of unselfishness and the ability to forgo individual ego and self-centered motives. The Gallop Partnership Scale is another useful theoretical framework for libraries to build successful community outreach and partnership programs and to seek tangible and nontangible support to strengthen library services.

Building Connection with Local Businesses

No matter how big or small, libraries can partner with local companies, businesses, and nonprofit enterprises with innovative services for their customers. Bigger cities' libraries such as Ohio's Cleveland Heights–University Heights Library (CHUHL) can partner with various local businesses: grocery stores, caterers, camera stores, toy stores, restaurants, vending machine companies, the art communities and relevant industries, and community events (Hakala-Ausperk, 2011). Rural and small libraries may have limited business partners in the community, maybe a local grocery store or a restaurant. Good connections means the library allows local businesses and organizations to market to its customers, and at the same time, the library enjoys improved patron services and financial well-being. In the end, both sides enjoy improved traffic and revenue. It is extremely important to keep good public relationships in a small community.

Some librarians are creative in dealing with library fines and choose to accept donations of food for fines instead. In this way, libraries gain returning patrons who no longer fear lost book and late return fines and maintain good relations in the community. Also a good marketing strategy, the food for fine program has been adopted by many libraries in recent years (http://eduscapes .com/marketing/13.htm).

Justifying Library Budget to Local Leaders

Libraries like to collect their circulation and use records for various evaluations and reporting purposes. It is valuable to research factors influencing the decision making on priorities of funding in the budgetary process. Public library stakeholders, such as municipal officials, elected council members, and mayors, may view the value of the data on library services differently than a library director. It is possible to see increased circulation numbers or user headcounts followed by a cut on library budgets. The theory of public choice explains that increased use does not result in increased funding (Stenström & Haycock, 2014).

Cialdini's theory of factors of influence (1993), as cited by Stenström and Haycock (2014), considers six factors that influence library budget decisions. These concepts are consistency and commitment, reciprocity, social proof, liking, scarcity, and authority. *Consistency and commitment* indicates that humans are deeply inclined to be consistent, hence if someone initially showed interest in a proposal when he or she was informed before, it is likely the person will support the proposal when it is put in a formal voting process. *Reciprocity* simply means humans like to trade favors among each other and don't want to feel indebted to others. *Social proof* means if lots of other people are doing something, then it will probably be OK to behave similarly. *Liking* means people are more likely to be influenced by people they like, for example, people like themselves, friends, and people they know and respect. *Scarcity* means things appear more attractive when their availability is limited or when a special offer will soon expire. *Authority* means people will be more likely to accept a proposal or buy a product if it is presented by a respected person.

Whenever there is a change in local political leadership, cost-saving plans, which can include a cut on library budgets, may emerge. It is the librarians' job to foresee local political change and potential impact to library funding and use all means, including the theoretical factors on influence to persuade the stakeholders to maintain library funding, not solely depending on their library's use of statistics.

Social Networking and Fundraising

Web-based environment and social media make the initial relationship building between a donor and an organization easy. Joseph and Lee (2012) presented a model of electronic fundraising and suggested the use of the model in libraries as nonprofit organizations (NPOs). They suggested a steady increase in online contributions to NPOs. The boom of social networking applications such as Facebook and Twitter are creating more points of contact between NPOs and donors. The increased use of social media also creates unique opportunities to attract an individual that is already online to donate to an organization that he/she is familiar with or believes in. NPOs can capitalize on the accessibility of the web and build relationships with current and future donors through e-mail, online event registration, and volunteer recruitment.

Electronic fundraising grabbed people's attention in the United States in the 2008 presidential election, when Barack Obama's campaign raised more funds from small-dollar fundraising though e-mail, social media, mobile devices, and its website during the race than through traditional fundraising methods (Scherer, 2012). This kind of fundraising is new to rural libraries, but libraries need to prepare for the future of this kind of e-fundraising. E-fundraising initiatives are online options to allow donors to use electronic payments. Common types of e-fundraising include printable forms, shopping carts that allow payment by credit and debit cards, and third party options such as PayPal, Apple Pay, and Google Checkout, and so on.

E-fundraising, or digital philanthropy as it is called by Price (2014), is still in its infancy but has foreseeable potential. The younger generations of library users, so called Millennials, are those who are born in the late 1970s through the early 2000s. This generation grew up in an age when information can be easily shared through a networked environment, and they feel comfortable contributing financially online. They are not dominate donors to public libraries yet, but in future years, today's younger generation will become tomorrow's established professionals with disposable income, as "Millennials age into respectability—and as they reveal themselves to be quite generous" (p. 172).

LIBRARIES AS NONPROFIT BUSINESS

Libraries nowadays often function as nonprofit businesses by providing nontangible services to users. In addition, a library can be a business partner. Cooperating with local businesses, library programs connect with local businesses or school band programs on mutually beneficial projects. Through the program, a library can build relationships with local businesses via helping these businesses to get more potential customers involved.

Unlike fully funded public libraries, small nonprofit libraries often receive partial funding from the city or country government, and nonprofit libraries have to raise funds to cover the rest of the cost. However, there might be legal issues for a government entity receiving private donations as a fully nonprofit business. Some libraries choose to remain a nonprofit business, but their local government is then not liable to fund them. Another challenge is the stability of leadership. The library donor database may not be available once a new library director is hired, if the previous director does not want to share the names of his/her library donors.

Thus, a more popular solution for rural libraries is to have a dedicated library fundraising foundation, or friends group, as a nonprofit business. Library affiliated nonprofit businesses can focus on a diversified fundraising plan that also includes strategies around major gifts, planned giving, legacy societies, and a strategic technology plan (Dillingham, 2013). Dillingham also listed names, budgets, and donations to major public libraries in big urban areas (http://www

.guidestar.org/downloadable-files/2013-public-libraries.pdf). He also found that almost 80% of the top 100 public libraries use a separate fundraising foundation, and the foundations vary in size and scope. Even if small libraries do not have the scale of big urban libraries and such businesses and donor bases, small town residents and businesses might be as philanthropic as their urban counterparts.

CONCLUSION

This chapter addressed funding sources from federal, local government, and nongovernment sources, as well as grant sources and grant agencies. Fundraising is one of the most important tasks that a rural library director faces every day. The chapter also addresses another important topic on how libraries justify their funding, so that a library's social impact can be demonstrated to stakeholders. Rural libraries need to work constructively with their local government agencies, possibly their biggest and most reliable funders. They also need to actively market themselves in order to collaborate with local businesses and other entities, serve the public good, and become mutually beneficial partners, particularly those libraries that fund themselves as non-profit businesses.

REFERENCES

American Library Association. (2006). Library fund raising: A selected annotated bibliography. Available at http://www.ala.org/Template.cfm?Section=Library_Fact_Sheets&Template=/ContentManagement/ContentDisplay.cfm&ContentID=25081

Benton, S. (2010). *Partners for the future: Public libraries and local governments creating sustainable communities.* Washington, DC: Urban Library Council. Available at http://www.urbanlibraries.org/filebin/pdfs/Sustainability_Report_2010.pdf

Bertot, J. C., Jaeger, P. T., Gorham, U., Taylor, N. G., & Lincoln, R. (2013). Delivering e-government services and transforming communities through innovative partnerships: Public libraries, government agencies, and community organizations. *Information Polity: The International Journal of Government & Democracy in the Information Age, 18*(2), 127–138.

Cialdini, R. B. (1993). *Influence: The psychology of persuasion* (Rev. ed.). New York: Williams Morrow.

Dillingham, W. J. (2013). *Public libraries in the United States: Overview & insights on library foundations.* New York: Wilmington Trust. Available at http://www.guidestar.org/downloadable-files/2013-public-libraries.pdf

Dowlin, K. (2008). *Getting the money: How to succeed in fundraising for public and nonprofit libraries.* Westport, CT: Libraries Unlimited.

Edwards, J. B., Rauseo, M. S., & Unger, K. R. (2013). Community centered: 23 reasons why your library is the most important place in town. *Public Libraries Online.* Available at http://publiclibrariesonline.org/2013/04/community-centered-23-reasons-why-your-library-is-the-most-important-place-in-town/

Farrell, M. (2012). *A brief history of national support for libraries in the United States*. Paper presented at IFLA World Library and Information Congress. Helsinki, Finland. Available at http://conference.ifla.org/ifla78

Fry, J. W. (1975). LIS and LSCA, 1956–1973: A legislative history. *Library Trends, 24,* 7–26.

Giesecke, J. (2012). The value of partnerships: Building new partnerships for success. *Journal of Library Administration, 52*(1), 36–52.

Gregory, G. M. (1999). The Library Services and Technology Act: How changes from LSCA are affecting libraries. *Public Libraries, 38*(6), 378–382.

Hakala-Ausperk, C. (2011). Waking up the neighborhood: Partnerships with local business and art communities. In K. Ellis (Ed.), *Partnerships and collaborations in public library communities: Resources and solutions* (pp. 15–23). Hershey, PA: IGI Global.

Hall, J. (2009). *Grant management: Funding for public and nonprofit programs*. Burlington, MA: Jones & Bartlett Learning.

Herring, M. Y. (2004). *Raising funds with friends groups: A how-to-do-it manual for librarians*. New York: Neal-Schuman.

Institute of Museum and Library Services. (2010). *State library administrative agencies survey: Fiscal year 2010*. Washington, DC: Institute of Museum and Library Services. Available at http://www.imls.gov/assets/1/AssetManager/stla2010.pdf

Kanter, R. M. (1994). Collaborative advantage: The art of alliances. *Harvard Business Review*. Available at https://hbr.org/1994/07/collaborative-advantage-the-art-of-alliances

Mackellar, P. H., & Gerding, S. K. (2010). *Winning grants: A how-to-do-in manual for librarians with multimedia tutorials and grant development tools*. Chicago, IL: American Library Association.

Merrifield, M. (1995). The funding of rural libraries. *Library Trends, 44*(1), 49–62.

Montiel-Overall, P. (2005). Toward a theory of collaboration for teachers and librarians. Available at http://www.ala.org/aasl/sites/ala.org.aasl/files/content/aaslpubsandjournals/slr/vol8/SLMR_TheoryofCollaboration_V8.pdf

O'Neal-McElrath, T. (2013). *Winning grants step by step: The complete workbook for planning, developing and writing success proposals*. San Francisco, CA: Jossey-Bass

Owens, P. L., & Sieminski, M. L. (2007). Local and state sources of funding for public libraries: The national picture. Available at http://www.pcblpa.org/Portals/8/Downloads/PaLALibraryFundingStudy.pdf

Price, L. (2014). Digital philanthropy and libraries. In M. S. Wood (Ed.), *Successful library fundraising: Best practices* (pp. 171–191). Lanham, MD: Rowman & Littlefield Publishers.

Public Library Quarterly. (2009). Library services for immigrants, an abridged version. *Public Library Quarterly, 28*(2), 120–126.

Scherer, M. (2012). Exclusive: Obama's 2012 Digital Fundraising Outperformed 2008. Time Magazine. Available at http://swampland.time.com/2012/11/15/exclusive-obamas-2012-digital-fundraising-outperformed-2008/

Stenström, C., & Haycock, K. (2014). Influence and increased funding in Canadian public libraries: The case of Alberta in fiscal year 2009–10. *The Library Quarterly, 84*(1), 49–68.

Swan, D. W., Grimes, J., Owens, T., Vese, R. D., Jr., Miller, K., Arroyo, et al. (2013). *Public libraries survey: Fiscal year 2010* (Report No. IMLS-2013-PLS-01).

Washington, DC: Institute of Museum and Library Services. Available at: https://www.imls.gov/publications/public-libraries-united-states-survey-fiscal-year-2010

Wagner, R., & Muller, G. (2009). *Power of 2: How to make the most of your partnerships at work and in life.* New York: Gallup Corporation.

Womack, L. (2012). Grant writing tips for beginners (Blog post). Available at http://arsl.info/2012/05/grant-writing-tips-for-beginners/

Wood, M. S. (2014). *Successful library fundraising: Best practices.* Lanham, MD: Rowman & Littlefield.

CHAPTER SEVEN

Using Outreach as a Marketing Tool

Many people don't take advantage of using public libraries in the United States. According to the 2013 Pew Research Center report (Zickuhr, Rainie, Purcell, & Duggan, 2013), 48% of Americans have visited a public library or bookmobile in the past 12 months, and 30% of Americans have visited a public library website. Among those who visited a public library or bookmobile in person in the last year, 43% said they visit the library less often than once a month. Shontz, Parker, and Parker (2004) suggested that one of the reasons for a low rate of library use might be that the librarians do not market themselves effectively. Many librarians do not have the knowledge of marketing, do not think marketing is important, or have a negative attitude toward marketing.

Our digital world brings many challenges to library marketing. Because potential users can go online anywhere and anytime, they do not have to come to a library building to access information. Libraries are not automatically considered the first place to go to find information, even though they may be situated in the central district of a town. As shown earlier with the Pew Report, many users today visit their physical library less often than in previous years. They are used to having instant access to information from search engines and are becoming less aware of what resources are available in libraries and how librarians can help their information access (Cole & Graves, 2010); at the same time, librarians are becoming more aware that they need to market themselves to founders, patrons, and the community. As Singh (2009) concluded in his survey report, having a positive attitude toward marketing is a prerequisite of the library leadership in order for the marketing oriented behavior of a library to be embraced. Finally, promoting a library's teen events and spaces to children and young users can be particularly beneficial, as they nowadays tend to distribute news quickly among themselves in social media. This chapter addresses the importance of marking library services and marketing strategies; marketing library resources and services is discussed as well as marketing to youth. The chapter concludes with the communication skills needed for library marketing.

THE IMPORTANCE OF LIBRARY MARKETING

Conventional thinking, that libraries are simply cultural and educational centers, could be a major reason that libraries need to be marketed to their users and potential users. The community needs to be reminded of the more practical services offered such as access to books, e-books, media, and reference services. Many public libraries are nonprofit organizations, and librarians must be made more aware of the importance of using marketing methods and techniques to promote their activities since financial resources are not enough, and the competition among agencies is fierce (Enache, 2008). As Masuchika (2013) suggested, there are a few ways that libraries can be more successful in their marketing. Never assume that libraries are the only option for information access within their community, as people get information from their local bookstores, the website Amazon.com, and the Internet. Masuchika also suggested letting free scholarly resources be available for research, including various digital resources across the Internet.

As stated above, librarians need to communicate with users regarding their products and services, which are more than just books, media, and reference services and which include programs, events, electronic resources, databases, and educational opportunities. Librarians further offer a service to help users find accurate information. As Dubichi (2007) commented, users rely more and more on electronic information over the Web, regardless of the authority of the information sources they locate. In our present digital environment, librarians must focus their efforts on marketing and promoting electronic resources and helping users to understand that what they are finding needs to be checked for authenticity and accuracy. This is just one of the services librarians offer in educating users as to what they can find in their libraries. Not only must librarians understand the need to market their services, but they must also have a plan for doing this. Germano (2010) concluded that the greatest obstacles to meaningful library marketing are a lack of vision, strategy, expectations, and expertise. The most important here seems to be "strategy."

MARKETING STRATEGIES

Librarians often do not have strategies or long-term plans for marketing. It is no secret that few librarians with this expertise are available, nor are they really sought after by library directors. A search against the American Library Association (ALA) joblist database (http://joblist.ala.org/) found virtually no marketing specialists positions advertised. In ALA accredited library schools, few offered courses specializing in library marketing. Creating a marketing strategy begins with a definition of marketing.

Definitions of Marketing

The American Marketing Association (2013) defines marketing as "the activity, set of institutions, and processes for creating, communicating, delivering, and exchanging offerings that have value for customers, clients, partners, and society at large." Alman and Swanson (2015) suggested that library marketing involves understanding of the community, identifying the services that they want or need, creating the services that will appeal to the user, and then effectively educating the users about these services. Marketing involves the following components: meeting the organization's mission, educating the users about programs and services, deciding on which programs and services that will best benefit the target audience, understanding the community, and advertising or outreach to the community (p. 2).

Outreach as a Marketing Strategy

With this objective in mind, librarians can apply outreach tools to gain community support. Outreach has a dual purpose here, not only used to provide information access to patrons who may not be able to come to the library but also used as a marketing tool to inform the public, build trust, better the reputation among the members of the community, and stay relevant to people's information needs. To achieve these goals, it is necessary to understand existing marketing strategies.

Williams (2013) promoted her library by outreach to new immigrants and adult literacy learners, as well as engaged a consultant to undertake a focus group interview, and then acted on the data gathered in order to make changes in services and policies. Librarians also collaborate with teachers and community workers based on their mutual interest in spreading the word about their library. Collaboration and outreach enables librarians to identify new service areas and spread the news of library services and resources to low-income and low-literacy residents.

Traditional marketing strategy in the business world focused on promoting tangible products such as automobiles, food, and even real estate properties. In the 1960s, E. Jerome McCarthy proposed a well-adopted marketing strategy using what has been coined "the 4Ps": product, price, place, and promotion (Waterschoot & van den Bulte, 1992; Dubichi, 2007). A product is used to satisfy what a consumer demands. The price determines the company's profit and existence. Promotion is the method of communication to make different parties aware of the product. Place is the distribution of the products for convenient consumer access.

In addition to McCarthy's 4Ps, 3 more Ps were added to the concept to include application to the service industry in which the library belongs: physical evidence, people, and process. Physical evidence shows the result and reassures the audience that the service took place, people are the employees who execute the services, and process determines how the procedure of a service product takes place. Libraries, like other nonprofit organizations, contribute to the society via value-added services rather than products to be sold for financial gain. The goal of library marketing is not to make a cash profit or "sell" any products. Libraries provide free public services for users to gain intellectual growth.

McCarthy's 4Ps can be used to promote one or more areas of library services. For example, Dubichi (2007) adopted the 4P marketing model in promoting libraries' electronic services. To her, the "products" are electronic resources as information services, the "price" is the convenience and the ease of the user experience when using electronic resources, and the "place" is online access through the library's website, either in the physical library or remotely from home, office, and school. She also recommended that a good marketing plan should incorporate input from both library staff and community users.

To promote library resources and services, it is a good idea to come up with a powerful short message or slogan as the promotional tool. This is easier for branding and allows patrons to remember quickly and recall the library's message. The promotion of library services will likely increase the library's visibility in the community, increase circulation counts, patron visits, library space use, and website traffic; however, these tangible results should not be the sole goals of library marketing. For a nonprofit organization, like a library, nontangible results such as community support and user loyalty would carry more emotional weight than would numbers and statistics, especially in digital era.

Other Marketing Strategies

Other marketing strategies include branding and rebranding with "touchpoints," service-based marketing, point-of-sale marketing, taking a leadership role, and improving the perception of the community for the value of library services. These are discussed below.

Libraries need to rebrand themselves; promote their resources, collections, and human talent; and reach out to community users. Some scholars defined the libraries as centers for "knowledge creation in their communities" (Lankes, 2011, p. 31; as cited in Grant, 2015). Librarians in small libraries should use this strategy also.

Singh and Ovsak (2013) commented that many librarians are rebranding the concept of a library by building positive images through "touchpoints," or the points of contact at which libraries serve their communities. They believe "it's important to recognize that a person's feelings about a library can be shaped through touchpoints such as word of mouth, the library's Web site and social media, databases, service encounters with library staff, and so on" (p. 345).

Adopting a service-based marketing strategy allows librarians to focus on the value that libraries represent, including the best access and delivery of relevant information in a timely way (Germano, 2010). Service-based marketing strategy is less concerned about the price and product and more focused on value, relationship loyalty, and the direct benefits to the user.

Masuchika (2013) suggested a "point-of-sale" marketing strategy for libraries. Point-of-sale is the location where currency is exchanged for goods and services in the business world. In library services, there are no monetary goods or services exchanged except for fines or fees, and the exchange is in the form of users receiving information services or accessing information resources. Point-of-sale events might happen in places such as the reference desk, circulation, or even as casual talk between librarians and local residents in and out of library buildings. Point-of-sale may be seen as the valuable face-to-face interaction needed in order to build trust and loyalty, the perception of the librarian in every environment users may see them. A loyal customer base for libraries is as important as a customer base for a commercial business that will close if it fails to make money during the exchange. A very practical point-of-sale strategy is the careful placement of materials in a visible area for patrons to find, such as a best sellers shelf or a "new additions" shelf. During televised events such as the Super Bowl or the Kentucky Derby, a collection of materials could be placed in an area near the circulation desk to attract users.

Another important strategy for library marketing is for librarians to take this opportunity to enhance their leadership skills. Not all librarians consider marketing in this way. The survey by Shontz, Parker, and Parker (2004) on librarians' attitudes toward marking found that administrators and public service librarians have a more positive attitude toward marketing than do reference and technical service librarians. Those who understand the importance of marketing tend to have previously attended courses, workshops, or training sessions in conferences or academic settings.

For a librarians to be more effective in marketing library services, librarians must constantly review the services they provide to satisfy user needs, eliminate services that are no longer needed, find the best way to make services accessible to a wide variety of patrons, reduce the service cost to patrons and the community, and make the public fully aware of the services and resources a library provides. A successful marketing strategy shows the value of the library in the community to the community.

MARKETING LIBRARY RESOURCES AND SERVICES

Libraries are interacting with the public all the time, and it is important to maintain the positive image of the community center. To do that, libraries need to actively inform and promote its resources and services to its communities. This section discusses promoting library resources and services, including digital promotion.

Promoting Library Resources

As stated earlier in the chapter, a traditional perception of libraries today is that they are a cultural and educational institution, which may also function as a kind of recreation center. This is often the case in public libraries, where patrons meet and greet and use common spaces to check out popular books.

Libraries, on the other hand, also try to be relevant by matching everything a bookstore can offer, including space, Wi-Fi, and even coffee. Library Wi-Fi is provided to users free of charge; usually there is no security authentication need to connect, but the service may be turned off after business hours. The library Wi-Fi services are funded through E-rate, which was discussed in previous chapters. The Wall Street Journal (Nagesh, 2014) reported that Federal Communication Commission (FCC) approved $1 billion annually to help schools and libraries connect to the Internet and deploy Wi-Fi services, while phasing out aging technologies such as pagers and landline phones. All these services have promoted library services successfully.

Two kinds of assets that a library can promote are the print and digital resources it acquires for the community to use for free, and the value-added services it provides to enhance education as well as to help local businesses grow. Pankl (2010) suggested that promoting library resources to local business makes the implicit promise that using them will always return a value to the user. Users are more appropriately considered to be "customers," who will gain a return on their investment of time and attention to library services, while at the same time being willing to contribute and subsidize the cost of a library. Librarians need to find out how to promote their resources and services by first finding out the needs of the local communities, which will be discussed in detail in chapter 10.

Another good way to promote library resources to the general public is to train all library staff members to be advocates of library resources. On one hand, librarians may be comfortable specializing in one or two areas of the library resources or services but find the amount of electronic resources overwhelming. Brannon (2007) initiated and managed the promotional campaign for the Denton Public Library's electronic databases after finding out that they had a consistent decline in the use of library electronic resources.

Not surprisingly, her library staff members reported that they themselves used databases only as their last resort. She started with training library staff on one database a day and made her staff feel comfortable with the electronic resources available, but even so, not all of them were willing to use the databases at first. After securing a small grant, they started a full-scale promotional plan ranging from pencils and pens distributions to middle school and high school visits, flyers, phone advertisements, and in-house training classes, among others. This achieved not only an increase in the use of library statistics but also reaffirmed the library's role in the community users' life-long learning. This also strengthened the library's outreach and community partnership with friends of the library, the chamber of commerce, and local businesses.

On the other hand, while many librarians are moving to promoting library resources and services electronically, it might be more efficient to also have a personal contact in the community so users can perceive that they have someone to approach when needed. They might be more likely to walk into the physical library when they have an information need if they know someone is there to answer questions. Nunn and Ruane (2012) used library reference services as the example and recommended this personalized marketing by linking users with not only just a building but also a face. Nunn and Ruane (2012) commented that for-profit companies have effectively demonstrated the impact of having a credible spokesperson to convey the quality of their service, and this technique can be one of the many ways that work for libraries as well (p. 576).

Traditional Marketing Venues

Librarians have many ways of traditionally promoting library resources and services to the community. Among these are posters and advertisements, commercial outlets and handouts, and word of mouth. Word of mouth as a marketing venue is still very efficient in small communities, and many librarians are efficient using it to promote library resources, services, and policies. The following are some marketing venues that worth considering:

Posters and Advertisements

Posters and advertisements are less effective methods to promote libraries that lack reputation, credibility, and trust among the community. The reputation of a library is based on previous successful cases where the library has proven that they have special resources fitting the customers' needs or on a staff's track record of helping a small business owner.

Commercial Media

Commercial media includes local radio, TV, and newspapers. These can be libraries' best friends and libraries should maintain a productive relationship with these media outlets. Featuring articles in local media can project a positive perception of library services and bring the attention of the community to events that are related to libraries. Press coverage may also enhance the sense of ownership from local community, thus making it very hard for stakeholders to reduce library budgets.

As mentioned above, rural libraries often find commercial media such as local newspapers, are one of their best marketing tools. Librarians can write articles, and sometimes they are posted on the front page of a newspaper. The UNT PEARL project found one of the common concerns from rural libraries today is that when librarians do not advertise, people tend to use library service less and less.

Handouts

Handouts are useful for people who want to have something tangible to read and pass around, assuming that they are well produced. If not, they are just papers and not something reinforcing the value of library resources and services, instead only adding to the piles of newspapers for recycling. Handouts should be well designed and contain information that a user might put on a bulletin board at their home or office. This would fulfill the library's marketing purpose. In recent years, some marketing specialists have experimented with handing out digital marketing media, for example, using USB jump drives with the library logo that inside contain information regarding library programs, events, and services. The cost of USB jump drives can come from the library's marketing budget or can be sponsored by a business partner. These are popular items and are more likely to be kept by the targeted audience.

In addition to library skills such as reference interviews, library instructions, and oral and written presentation skills, small libraries may need extra players, even pets, to attract community attention and enhance their public relations and marketing efforts. For example, not only did the story of Dewey the Library Cat (Myron & Witter, 2008) from Spencer, Iowa, resonate with book lovers and capture their imagination from all around the world, but also transferred their kind feelings toward the animal to the library and transformed this small town to its current success (http://www.deweyreadmorebooks.com/).

Digital Promotion

While for-profit businesses set up online shops and have been successful in advertising their products or driving customers to their brick-and-wall stores, libraries can also use digital media to promote their intangible resources and services in communities too. With the explosion of computer and mobile Web access, it is common to see libraries utilize online marketing and rely on social media to promote their resources and services.

The rationale of online marketing is that, as discussed throughout this chapter, many users today tend to use search engines to access information and thus visit their physical library less frequently. They like to have instant access to the information that they want, and this makes the multiple channels of marketing more important, because such users may grow less aware of the value and services offered by the library. Duncan (2009) commented that electronic library marketing does not necessarily mean transcribing traditional marketing materials to an electronic version but does instead mean reinventing and redesigning in order to create a new marketing format, with the purpose of targeting users and nonusers, to understand their needs, while also monitoring closely the results needed to maintain the library's relevancy in a digital world. The example of an e-newsletter, which is an e-mail-based electronic message, could be sent with high community relevance and low frequency of issues, to promote library events and activities.

Web or Online Marketing

Digital online marketing, such as websites, blogs, wikis, Facebook, Twitter, e-mail, instant messaging (IM), mobile chat, and text messaging, can be an effective way to communicate with the new generation of users today. E-mails are a convenient way to pass along information about library programs to communities. Facebook and Twitter allow libraries to use social networks to exchange information with potential users in a split-second of time. Social networking communications are inexpensive and efficient ways to promote library information to community users, as well as make it possible for librarians to get involved in community events.

Social Media

Social media platforms, such as Facebook, Twitter, Google+, YouTube, and LinkedIn, are building virtual communities that bring people together on the Internet. Social media channels potentially provide libraries with a direct connection to their customers with little or no cost, especially if the librarian is creative when producing digital content (Dankowski, 2013). When an organization utilizes Facebook, they can create Facebook pages on behalf of the organization, a function similar to webpages. For new users, Facebook asks the organization to register and complete a user "Profile," which contains date of birth, gender, marital status, and so on. King (2011) recommended that a team of librarians is needed in order to maintain a library's social networking sites, so that the library can adequately cover the day's interactions with users, as well as have fun.

King (2015) suggested that librarians need to shift communication channels and communication skills for library marketing and share traditional library-related activities in these new spaces, for example, answering questions from followers in the community, having casual conversations with library patrons, promoting library services in social media, and sharing library classes and events. King (2015) commented below on how a library should promote to its community:

> You might create posters and hang them in your building. You can do a similar thing online, using social media tools. For example, you can create a Facebook event and post about the event in other social media channels. You can create a video about a new library service and share that video using Facebook and Twitter. The upside to this? You are sharing about a new service or event with people who have "signed up" to see those promotional pieces.

Promoting libraries in social media draws attention to the need for communication skills, which is not emphasized in traditional library and information curriculum. A librarian's information searching skills may not directly translate to the interpersonal and intercultural communication that is taking place in social networks. This requires librarians not only to be able to promote positive images of their libraries to social media but also to deal with possible negative feedback online, as Bokor (2014) called, the "brand destruction" power online. Any brand name can potentially be attacked by opinion leaders, by a consumer group, or by Internet users, especially under a real-time, instant communication even among physically distributed communities. Since social networking sites don't really verify the actual age of users, both children and adults can publish opinions on issues of their interests. This makes it more necessary for libraries to maintain good online communications with all user age groups in their communities.

MARKETING TO YOUTH

The youth is a special group of people that need a special strategy when promoting the libraries. They actively share information and do not want to be left behind among peers.

Urquhart (2013) suggested ideas and strategies for promoting libraries to teens. She recommended the first step of marketing to teens be to build trust. Since teens are in the stage of becoming independent thinkers, they like to see libraries as being credible when it comes time to promote something tangible. Close relationships are cultivated the same way, as people engage in social media with their friends, such as sharing something funny, posting photos, and commenting on other people's posts, tweets, and photos.

It is very important to dedicate youth space in libraries. Bourke (2009) reviewed literature on youth spaces and saw increased dedicated library space for young users. One of the specific trends in recent years is to include electronic games and entertainment—Wii, Xbox, and PlayStation—in order to encourage young people to use the library. There is not enough data to know how many of these users become lifelong learners because of these facilities, but one can safely conclude that having dedicated space and games for the youth is a good marketing action toward the youth. This will help them to socialize with friends, reflect their own identity, feel a sense of ownership, and spread the word about library services and resources. More on teen space is discussed in chapter 9.

In-house marketing events can focus on one popular music title such as *Creatures of the Night* to attract teen readers, for example, can focus on a special cookbook and organize cooking contest events, or can focus on technology events using nonfiction books as vehicles of information, such as computers, gaming, and other technologies for the topics. Other ways of marketing to youth include library visits to local schools to let students know the library activities, as well as visits to local teen hangouts places. Campbell and Dunn (2008) recommended creative ways of marketing library reading programs to youth, for example in-branch ideas such as displays and booklists, outreach ideas such as flyers and school or community visits, and virtual outreach through blogs, wikis, and social networking tools.

Interaction with teens through social media extends the representation of librarians through social media. This channel can also be used to promote the profession of librarianship to younger generations to help them to understand that libraries are not only a gateway to the world of knowledge but also a profession that educates the public and supports the lifelong learning of all citizens in their communities.

Mobile access allows broader information access to children and the youth. A national survey (Nanji, 2013) showed that 75% of American children under 8 years of age have access to some type of "smart" mobile device, such as a smartphone or a tablet, in 2013, versus only 52% in 2011; American adults who upgraded their mobile devices probably passed their old devices to their children for entertainment, learning, or communication. It is also interesting to see that differences of income levels no longer play an important role for youth to have access to mobile devices. In 2011, only 22% of low-income children had access on mobile smart devices, versus 65% in 2013. Access to digital devices permits libraries to create youth-oriented programs and to promote to youth and their families using various texts, newsfeeds, photo sharing, and social media announcements.

COMMUNICATION SKILLS FOR LIBRARY MARKETING

As cited in this chapter, Alman (2005) suggested that library marketing includes the planning and developing stages, communicating to the community using commercial media, and using social media. To be more effective at library marketing, librarians need to have good personal communication skills, including written, oral, nonverbal communications (Stueart & Moran, 2007, p. 367). Written communication can be flawed and misunderstood. Among written communications, e-mails can make it "frighteningly easy to get into conflicts" because of the "generally hasty, ill-considered, and uncrafted nature of electronic communication" (Stueart & Moran, 2007, p. 368).

While the individual writing skills may not improve in a short period of time, there are abundant sources for writing a marketing plan. Lavingsky (2013) presented marketing plan templates in business perspectives and identified key points that need to be address, such as target customers, marketing strategies, and customer retention. Identify target customers will help to pinpoint the promotion effort and to understand target customers' concerns. At the same time, marketing plans identify marketing materials and promoting strategy; both need strong communication skills to communicate with the customer (http://www.forbes.com/sites/davelavinsky/2013/09/30/marketing-plan-template-exactly-what-to-include/3/).

Oral communication, both with individuals or groups, is considered rich in information. Oral communication can still be ambiguous, but it can be clarified with follow-ups. Oral communication can be time-consuming while the discussed content can be forgotten if not preserved.

Stueart and Moran (2007) defined nonverbal communication as "any type of communication that is not spoken or written" (p. 369). Eye contact and facial expression are examples of nonverbal communication. They may add more information to verbal communication. However, in some cultures direct eye contact is considered inappropriate, so nonverbal communication should be interpreted carefully.

CONCLUSION

This chapter focused on outreach as a marketing tool and the importance of library marketing. It discussed various marketing strategies and stressed promoting library resources and services both in traditional and digital manners. Some special factors to take into consideration when marketing to teens and youth were identified. The critical nature of communication skills when marketing the library was addressed.

In addition to face-to-face interactions, library staff must be competent in communicating using digital media. Librarians must acknowledge there is a gap between those who might not have the technology skills or the access to digital communication. The next chapter will discuss how to bridge this gap.

REFERENCES

Alman, S. W., & Swanson, S. G. (2015). *Crash course in marketing for libraries.* Santa Barbara, CA: ABC-CLIO.

American Marketing Association. (2013). Definition of marketing. Available at https://www.ama.org/AboutAMA/Pages/Definition-of-Marketing.aspx

Bokor, T. (2014). More than words—Brand destruction in the online sphere. *Budapest Management Review, 45*(2), 40–45.

Brannon, S. (2007). A successful promotion campaign: We can't keep quiet about our electronic resources. *The Serials Librarian, 53*(3), 41–55.

Cole, K., & Graves, T. (2010). Marketing the library in a digital world. *The Serials Librarian, 58,* 182–187. doi:10.1080/03615261003625729

Dubichi, E. (2007). Basic marketing and promotion concepts. *The Serials Librarian, 53*(3), 5–15.

Duggan, M. (2013). *Photo and video sharing grow online.* Washington, DC: Pew Research Center. Available at http://www.pewinternet.org/2013/10/28/photo-and-video-sharing-grow-online/

Duncan, R. (2009). Smarketing: Smarter marketing for libraries. *Australasian Public Libraries and Information Services, 22*(4), 149–156.

Enache, I. (2008). The theoretical fundamentals of library marketing. *Philobiblon: Transylvanian Journal of Multidisciplinary Research in Humanities, 13,* 477–490.

Germano, M. A. (2010). Narrative-based library marketing: Selling your library's value during tough economic times. *The Bottom Line: Managing Library Finances, 23*(1), 2010, 5–17.

Grant, C. (2015). It's time to define a new brand for libraries. Let's make sure it leaves people soaring, not snoring. *Public Library Quarterly, 34*(2), 99–106.

King, D. L. (2011). Facebook for libraries. *American Libraries* (Blog Post). Available at http://americanlibrariesmagazine.org/2011/05/27/facebook-for-libraries/

King, D. L. (2015). Why use social media? *Library Technology Reports, 51*(1), 6–9.

Lankes, D. (2011). *The atlas of new librarianship.* Cambridge, MA: MIT Press.

Masuchika, G. (2013). The reference desk, points-of-sale, and the building of loyalty: Applications of customer relationship management techniques to library marketing. *The Reference Librarian, 54*(4), 320–331.

Myron, V., & Witter, B. (2008). *Dewey: The small-town library cat who touched the world.* New York: General Central.

Nagesh, G. (2014). FCC votes to provide Wi-Fi to schools, libraries. *Wall Street Journal.* Available at http://www.wsj.com/articles/fcc-votes-to-provide-wi-fi-to-schools-libraries-1405107120

Nanji, A. (2013). *75% of American children under 8 have access to a smartphone or tablet.* Dover, DE: MarketingProfs LLC. Available at http://www.marketingprofs.com/charts/2013/12042/75-of-american-children-under-8-have-access-to-a-smartphone-or-tablet

Nunn, B., & Ruane, E. (2011). Marketing gets personal: Promoting reference staff to reach users. *Journal of Library Administration, 51*(3), 571–580.

Pankl, R. R. (2010). Marketing the public library's business resources to small business. *Journal of Business & Finance Librarianship, 15,* 94–103.

Shontz, M. L., Parker, J. C., & Parker, R. (2004). What do librarians think about marketing? A survey of public librarian's attitudes toward the marketing of library services. *Library Quarterly, 74*(1), 63–84.

Singh, R. (2009). Does your library have an attitude problem towards "marketing"? Revealing inter-relationship between marketing attitudes and behavior. *Journal of Academic Librarianship, 35*(1), 25–32.

Singh, R., & Ovsak, A. (2013). Library experience matters! Touchpoints to community engagement. *Journal of Library Administration, 53,* 344–358.

Urquhart, C. (2013). Top ten tips for marketing to teens. *Young Adult Library Services, 12*(1), 20.

Waterschoot, W., & van den Bulte, C. (1992). The 4P classification of the marketing mix revisited. *Journal of Marketing, 56*(4), 83–93.

Williams, K. (2013). Beyond books: Outreach at Winnipeg Public Library. *Feliciter, 59*(2), 19–22.

Zickuhr, K., Rainie, L., Purcell, K., & Duggan, M. (2013). *How Americans value public libraries in their communities.* Washington, DC: Pew Internet Research. Available at http://libraries.pewinternet.org/2013/12/11/section-1-an-overview-of-americans-public-library-use/

CHAPTER EIGHT

Bridging the Digital Divide

"Digital divide" is an official term that was coined in the 1990s by the Clinton/Gore administration. It refers to the social gap between those who have access to and use computers and the Internet and those who do not have computers or the Internet. Efforts made to lessen the breadth of the digital divide resulted in the connection of U.S. school classrooms to the Internet, and these efforts have become a cornerstone concept in building and improving the information technology infrastructure in the United States, which presently covers urban, suburban, and rural areas. Lots of progress has been made, particularly with high-speed Internet found in schools and public libraries.

This chapter will describe the digital divide in the United States, possible reasons leading to digital divide, the role of the library in trying to close the digital divide, e-government services, the library providing education to overcome the digital divide, and economic issues, followed by a discussion of broadband and mobile services.

DIGITAL DIVIDE IN THE UNITED STATES

Today, the digital divide remains a concern in many parts of the United States. This section will address the status of digital divide in the United States and possible reasons leading to various forms of digital divide.

Status of the Digital Divide

The last U.S. Census revealed that of the households earning $25,000 or less, 48.4% have paid subscriptions to the Internet (File & Ryan, 2014, p. 4). Students cannot survive without having access to the Internet in this modern age, in order to do homework and check e-mails, and both parents and students need to be able to check grades online. Because almost all job applications are online, an individual cannot apply for a job without access to the Internet to download, complete, and return the application. Despite the increased access to Internet in homes and via mobile devices, for a surprising number of people, including the poor, elderly, undereducated, and many minorities, cyberspace is still an inaccessible, often dimly perceived realm that is tangled with real life (Warf, 2012). It is ironic that, in the United States, many who enjoy reliable access to the Internet can read digital books, share digital content online, play online games, and probably address the issue of information overload, while many other citizens are deprived of similar access to knowledge, gained through e-books and information, which includes the ability to apply for jobs and many other necessities and conveniences.

According to 2014 Pew Research, 87% of American adults use the Internet (http://www.pewinternet.org/data-trend/internet-use/latest-stats/). Today, the many gaps among Internet users seem to be disappearing. The differences among genders, races or ethnicities, and community types are minimal, while differences among age groups, education levels, and household incomes are still large. While 88% of people 18–64 use the Internet, send or receive e-mail, or access the Internet via a mobile device, only 57% of people 65 or older use the Internet. A much lower percentage, 77%, of households with incomes of $30,000 per year or less use Internet, compared with 93% of households with incomes of $50,000 or more. For many, this makes the library the place for Internet access and a central location to get training; the library is an anchor in public broadband access in communities. As a place that serves the information needs of every users in the community, libraries help to decrease this gap.

Possible Reasons Leading to the Digital Divide

Warf (2012) reviewed the state of the digital divide in the United States and found that a large number of people—the poor, the elderly, the undereducated, and many minorities—consider cyberspace an inaccessible and often dimly perceivably realm. The 71 million nonusers of the Internet in the United States are diverse: one-quarter never completed high school, roughly one-fifth live with someone who does have Internet at home or work, and another 17% of nonusers are "Internet dropouts," typically those who are not happy with their computer hardware, software, or Internet service provider (ISP). Some fear the Internet due to pornography, privacy violations, credit fraud, and identify theft. Another one-quarter of nonusers struggle with literacy problems, and they are even less likely than are other nonusers to use their library's public Internet services.

Information needs of different income levels are divided, too. The interest in informative content to low-income individuals is different from mid-income or higher income people. Plumb (2007) commented that many of the households experiencing the digital divide have no or little extra money, and they therefore have little interest in shopping, travel, and recreational information. For many, relevant content means practical and local helpful information, such as low-cost childcare, free legal services, or job-training programs. For immigrants and people with low English-literacy skills, relevant information means materials written in basic English or in languages other than English, including information such as tax forms, social security documents, and medical and health care information.

Geographical location is another factor that contributes to digital divide. For example, rural area Internet access is particularly difficult because the populations are broadly distributed and are frequently poorer, older, and less educated than those in urban areas. This not only makes it harder for rural areas to generate economies of scale, but because of the perceived lesser income levels and smaller user groups, ISPs do not have the incentives to deploy modern infrastructure, such as fiber optic cables, in rural communities.

Warschauer (2003) has cautioned that a digital divide is marked not only by physical access to computers and connectivity but also by access to the additional resources that allow people to use technology. In essence, the physical availability of computers and connectivity is still critical, but more important issues are found in the digital content, language, education level, and literacy of the community and the social resources, all of which are difficult to overcome in people's minds.

Warschauer (2003) also cited personal communication with Rob Kling, director of the Center for Social Informatics at Indiana University, to provide greater details of the importance of social aspects rather than just of the physical connectivity:

> [The] big problem with "the digital divide" framing is that it tends to connote "digital solutions," i.e., computers and telecommunications, without engaging the important set of complementary resources and complex interventions to support social inclusion, of which informational technology applications may be enabling elements, but are certainly insufficient when simply added to the status quo mix of resources and relationships. (p. 7)

Thus, the digital divide cannot be solved solely by building more information technology infrastructures in remote and rural areas, a solution also requires an investment in information services, such as language training, reading, and literacy, and an understanding of the divided people's information needs, and many of these services are provided by rural libraries.

ROLE OF LIBRARIES IN CLOSING THE DIGITAL DIVIDE

Digital divide will be an ongoing problem in modern society as long as there are socioeconomic differences among countries, communities, and citizens. Even in the United States, the most powerful country, there are 25 million households (21%) that have no regular Internet access at all, either at home or elsewhere (Rainne & Cohn, 2014; Baker, 2015).

Libraries are designed to safeguard the knowledge of a society and to share it with all residents. With the same philosophy, digital era libraries should have programs designed to provide total access to the collection, and an easy delivery to reach those users whose access may be restricted by issues such as income, education, region, disability, age, gender, and race. Successful libraries in the digital age may partner with local vendors, including businesses and government agencies, in order to add service values to patrons, to be sustainable, and to make sure the libraries have collections in multiple formats.

Digital Divide and Information Access

Baker (2015) pointed that the people in the 25 million households without Internet access may not have a computer at home, may have limited computer stills, and may not know they can get online at their local library. Baker emphasized how library staff should spend a good amount of time with one patron on a particular website.

Many people use libraries' computer hardware and their connections to access the Internet. The use the library Internet improves community users' literacy skills and bridges the digital divide. An impact can be seen throughout a large part of the community due to their library's investment in the hardware needed in order to access the Internet, including Wi-Fi availability at the library for those with computers but no Wi-Fi at home. The availability of other communication technologies in the library will naturally lead to a greater return on investment from the communities. The library outreach services to senior citizens for training to use the Internet and computer technologies will also yield a broader impact. As an IMLS (Institute of Museum and Library Services, 2004, p. 4) report summarized:

> Public library computers are reaching the disadvantaged groups consistently identified as lacking technology access and skills. To a greater extent than the general population, certain ethnic groups and people with lower income and education levels rely on library computers as their only means of accessing computers and the Internet. The reliance is even more pronounced with children and adolescents in these disadvantaged groups.

The same report also suggested that library computers are helping patrons communicate, learn, work, and create. Libraries are the Internet providers for communities.

Libraries as Internet Providers

As Kinney (2010) stated, provision of Internet access is only one part of bridging the digital divide, which is a function of broader social and technological inequities. Access to public libraries is not sufficient to remedy broad social inequities, as there are disparities among library systems between urban, suburban, and rural libraries. Among all of them, rural libraries have the least amount of funding, staff training, and access to up-to-date infrastructure. Access to library computers is not as convenient as access in home and may not be beneficial to those who are the most disadvantaged. Equal access to the Internet, if without equal participation from low-income users, does not mean equal outcomes.

In a Pew Research report (Zickuhr, Raine, & Purcell, 2013) on a survey of 2,252 Americans 16 years and older on what people think is important for libraries to offer, 80% of respondents believe "librarians to help people find information" is important; only 16% said they are "somewhat important." For "free access to computers and Internet," 77% said very important, while 18% chose to answer "somewhat important." (p. 42). On "Job/career resources," 67% selected "very important" in their survey, versus the 22% who selected "somewhat important" (http://libraries.pewinternet.org/2013/01/22/part-4-what-people-want-from-their-libraries/, p. 40). This demonstrates that libraries provide more than just access; to many, the library is the only Internet provider that is available to them. This is particularly true in rural and remote areas.

For instance, 19 % of rural libraries have Internet speeds of 1.5 megabits per second or slower, as opposed to only 2% of urban libraries (Delaney, 2014; Bertot, Jaeger, Lee, Debbels, McDermott, & Real, 2014). Even though the Internet speed is slower in rural libraries, patrons can still enjoy subsidized and faster E-rate Internet connections in libraries than household Internet connections, as their household speeds still lag behind the national average.

Virtually every public library in the United States provides public access to the Internet via computers as a central part of its mission. Internet access can provide economic benefits, both indirectly, through the development of a marketable workforce, and directly through Internet-based businesses (Kinney, 2010). In addition to business potential, the information access can also help people to find health-related information and potentially save big on medically related costs. To low-income communities, free Internet access means residents can divert their financial resources to more important items, such as food and education. One of the successful cases is the Delta County Library, in Colorado (Delaney, 2014). Previously, at nighttime, cars parked outside, in the library parking lot, in order to use the free Wi-Fi. With a grant called the WhiteSpace Pilot, the library built a community-based free Wi-Fi system on the main street and in the town park. Anyone with a mobile device can find the library's hotspot and access the Internet.

The role of libraries in Internet access is a factor that influences the outcome of user participation. Many users treat the library's free Internet access as an extension of its traditional role in terms of the gateway of information and knowledge, while others treat the library as a safe community common space where they can do research and enhance their literacy skills. To some, the Internet might encroach on the library's role as a provider of reader's advisory services, online databases, and current information, but libraries are still unique because they provide programming activates for adults and children; they also offer outreach to users who may not be able to come to the library, and they also provide a place to meet and greet people from the same community (Vavrek, 2000; Rodger, D'Elia, & Jörgensen, 2001). As Kinney (2010) commented:

> Access alone is not enough to remedy technological inequities. Public access is not of the same quality as home access; access does not ensure effective use; and broader social and economic issues hamper the ability of access to remedy social ills. Libraries currently go beyond access by providing training, outreach, and content development, but many do not have the resources to provide these services at a high level . . . Internet assistance and training provided by staff are very important: they are a natural extension of libraries' information literacy role, they are how libraries stand out from other providers of Internet access, and they will continue to be relevant as technology changes. (p. 148)

Library and E-government Services

E-government is defined by the United Nations as "the employment of the Internet and the world-wide-web for delivering government information and services to the citizens" (United Nations, 2006, p. 1). E-government information service is a special kind of support for information access by libraries, and it is especially relevant in rural areas.

Libraries can help residents learn how to access their local city or county websites to pay their utility bills, find out how to get a building permit, register for business licenses, look at their property tax records, or determine where to vote in a local election. Library users can learn how to register to vote in state or federal elections. E-government information services may also include finding information on legal issues such as child custody, name change, and social security benefits.

E-government is relevant to local government also because many of the political processes are taking place online, for example, social media outreach including Facebook and Twitter, e-mail distribution lists, political campaigns, and fundraising. Those who are divided either feel uncomfortable or don't know the venues of participating in the political process online. This will have a long-term social-economic impact on the divided and will contribute to the potential loss of education and employment opportunities in the long run.

Government initiatives focusing on Internet access may not solve all of the problems related to the digital divide. Stevenson (2009, p. 1) pointed out that "by concentrating primarily on the problem of access to the technology, state programs designed to bridge the digital divide have failed ultimately to improve the lives of those who might benefit from them the most." She commented that "the so-called digitally divided may not even be using public access computing (PAC) services, whether are offered through a public library or a community technology center." (pp. 1-2). The emphasis is for libraries to facilitate and conduct user education on access and training in the digital world, not simplified as just an investment on hardware and connections.

Digital Literacy Training for Bridging the Divide

The American Library Association (ALA) digital literacy task force (Visser, 2012. http://connect.ala.org/node/181197) defines digital literacy as "the ability to use information and communication technologies to find, evaluate, create, and communicate information, requiring both cognitive and technical skills". Digital literacy emphasizes:

- personal learning skills and technical skills,
- the ability to use computer and appropriate technologies to communicate with other people in the society, and
- the ability to protect personal privacy.

Digital literacy training enhances library users' learning skills. Librarians in their communities are also teachers/trainers and information service providers on the topics of health care, finances, education, job seeking, community participation, gaming, and other individualized information seeking topics (Kinney, 2010; McClure & Jaeger, 2009). Library training may lead them to realize the authority of information resources and may assist users to begin to use the library electronic resources. The Internet has expanded the roles and services of libraries in bridging the digital divide. Rural public libraries should recognize this dual role of "Internet providers" and "technological trainers and educators" and publicize the importance of such services to funders, users, and stakeholders across and beyond communities. Since a majority of websites related to daily work and entertainment are in the English language, basic language skill is necessary to navigate online. Language literacy is the individual skill of being able to read and write, as well as being able to gather, comprehend, and make use of information from a variety of sources (Eisenstein, 1979, as cited in Warschauer, 2003). Having reading literacy is not just an option these days but a requirement. Libraries that provide technology and reading literacy classes to its residents are probably providing the long-term solution to bridge the digital divide in rural communities.

Digital literacy training also includes technical training including computer skills. Computer skills are needed to search online job listings, compile one's resume, and fill out online job application forms. A recent news report stated that 80% of all U.S. jobs will require digital fluency within the next 10 years and that 80% of Fortune 500 companies only accept job applications online. College applications, financial aid, and even registration and classwork itself have all moved online (http://www.detroitnews.com/story/opinion/2015/05/26/america -closes-digital-divide/27785259/). At the same time, studies show that many dysfunctional job application websites are complicated, confusing, and very hard to complete (Baker, 2015). Libraries are also known to teach free digital literacy courses and are helping the job growth for immigrants and low-income citizens. Job seekers often consult with libraries on websites, on books and materials on creating resumes, and for training users on computers.

Digital literacy also includes the ability to evaluate the content over the Internet and protect a user's own privacy information. Plumb (2007) warned librarians to make the divided user groups aware of the privacy issues and risky Internet behavior, which means that a public user training session may include training on the differences seen between entering personal information in an unknown .com or .net website as opposed to a .gov or .edu site. Training should also contain appropriate ways to react to spamming, spyware, cookies, and security software, in order to build confidence in the users' ability to surf the Web safely. Chapter 10 discusses more on Internet and data security.

It is a challenging task for public libraries to train various people from different skill levels and cultural background, often with various reading, writing, and cognitive thinking skills. At the same time, the formal and informal education to community users from libraries plays an important role in how to use the Internet and what benefits are gained from it (Warschauer, 2003, p. 109). Instead of teaching everyone with the same literacy program, public librarians may need to treat individuals with different literacy levels with a different instruction strategy.

Unlike in traditional environments, many libraries today are serving new types of users that are both content consumers and producers (James, 2009). As digital content consumers, many Internet users enjoy browsing Instagram photos, watching YouTube videos, and checking the updates from Facebook or Twitter, but they might also participate in posting the photos, making the videos, and pushing the updates on Facebook, Twitter, and Pinterest. Being a digital content consumer may encourage them to be digital content producers in today's social-networking sites. At the same time, digital content creation such as video production requires a broadband Internet to upload and download data. The next section discussed broadband Internet issues.

BROADBAND INTERNET ISSUES

A 2010 U.S. news source reported that back in 2004, Netflix, the Internet video-streaming-service company, had threatened the existence of Blockbuster, the biggest video rental business. New technology defeated the old one in just a few years (Newman, 2010). Today, thanks to broadband Internet in many parts of the world, Netflix has 65.55 million subscribers, with 42.3 million in the United States and 23.25 million internationally (Udland, 2015).

As Internet traffic has increased due to the rich graphic content, access to broadband is becoming more important, since more and more people use broadband Internet to access Netflix and digital television programs, voice over Internet protocol (VoIP) telephone, business-to-business communications, Internet-based multipleplayer role-playing video games, telemedicine, and video conferencing services and tools. More and more people save files and important materials to the cloud-based computing such as Dropbox. Warf (2012) also concluded that broadband delivery forms the new era of the digital divide in the

United States, especially between urban and rural communities. While gender does not make a difference in broadband accessibility, income, age, educational level, and rural and urban location are prime determinants of who uses broadband and who does not. A White House report (Council of Economic Advisers, 2015, p. 1) emphasized that the "'digital divide' is concentrated among older, less educated, and less affluent populations, as well as in rural parts of the country that tend to have fewer choices and slower connections." Librarians should understand that rural America and underserved populations may be marginalized if broadband issue are not address. This section analyzes economic issues related to broadband Internet, followed by a discussion of bridging the gap of broadband in rural areas.

Economic Issues and the Digital Divide

Americans pay more for their Internet access than European countries, according to the 2014 annual report released by the New America Foundation's Open Technology Institute (http://www.newamerica.org/oti/the-cost-of-connectivity-2014/). For example, Internet users in Seoul continue to get the speediest connections at the lowest prices anywhere in the world, with speeds of one gigabit per second costing just $30 a month, while by contrast, the best speeds that consumers in Los Angeles, Washington, DC, or New York can get are half as fast and cost $300 a month.

A congressional research service report (Kruger & Gilroy, 2013) defined the issue as the effect of scales on economy on the difficulties of developing rural broadband:

> The comparatively lower population density of rural areas is likely the major reason why broadband is less deployed than in more highly populated suburban and urban areas. Particularly or wireline broadband technologies—such as cable modem and DSL—the greater the geographical distances among customers, the larger the cost to serve those customers. Thus, there is often less incentive for companies to invest in broadband in rural areas than, for example, in an urban area where there is more demand (more customers with perhaps higher incomes) and less cost to wire the market area. (p. 7) (https://www.fas.org/sgp/crs/misc/RL30719.pdf)

As mentioned in chapter 4, in public infrastructure buildings, an interesting phenomenon is that locally owned Internet providers continue to be competitive. The New America Foundation's (2014) report highlighted the fact that city-owned networks are becoming more competitive with the offerings from Internet providers around the world. The small number of towns that have built such networks—like Chattanooga, Tennessee, and Lafayette, Louisiana—ranked higher in their reports on speed and price than almost every other city except for those in Asia. While there are many local legislature barriers on government-owned business, in general, it seems that these locally owned networks tend to deliver better value to their customers when compared, on a price-per-megabit basis, to competing cable and telecom providers in their own cities (http://www.huffingtonpost.com/2014/10/31/internet-speeds_n_6078204 .html). However, much still has to be done on researching how to balance free market principles, fair business practices, and competition from government-funded projects on local broadband construction.

Broadband in Rural Areas

Broadband access brings opportunities to low-income and low-education level individuals because they are the greatest in need; the Internet will bring them information concerning job opportunities, bus schedules, and even comparison shopping. These lower income and literacy level people are tomorrow's labor force, and they will largely influence the national competition of the United States in the global market environment.

Broadband services are the current format of the digital divide in the Unites States. As Warf suggested, government funding and initiatives are still essential to bridge the gap, to found the E-rate program, to provide high-speed access to public schools and libraries, and to provide training on software to teachers and librarians. Subsidies are needed on projects such as community public Wi-Fi hotspots, so the inhabitants of remote and impoverished residential areas at least have a place to apply for job applications, follow the social media, and engage in political discussions with minimum or no cost. At the same time, it is obvious many libraries, particular rural and small libraries, do not have enough resources, enough physical spaces, and enough human power to accommodate all user needs. As an IMLS report suggested: "The physical infrastructure of libraries significantly limits the number of public access computer terminals that can be accommodated, but libraries are also limited by their technology infrastructure and their ability to maintain the equipment they have in good working order" (Becker et al., 2011, p. 101), and some expand their services to wireless Internet access for users with their own computers.

MOBILE SERVICES AND DIGITAL DIVIDE

Some aspects of the digital divide may disappear when certain technologies saturate the market. For example, dial-up Internet can cover the areas where broadband access is not available. In recent years, the iPhone and Android smart phones have gained tremendous popularity in the United States and around the world. Mobile phones, particularly with Internet data plans, enable people to access the Internet without the limitation of the location of the housing and communities, as well as service map limitation from the ISPs. This mobility also enables younger generations to be updated with technology and engage in social media and political events. A recent report from the *New York Times* found that mobile technologies are bridging the gap of divide (http://bits.blogs .nytimes.com/2009/07/22/mobile-internet-use-shrinks-digital-divide/?_r=0).

They found that nearly half of all African Americans and English-speaking Hispanics (the study did not include a Spanish-language option) were using mobile phones or other handheld devices to surf the Web and send e-mail messages. By comparison, just 28% of white Americans reported ever going online using a mobile device.

A survey by Pearce and Rice (2013) found a similar pattern in an international study, comparing mobile Internet users from the United States and those from Republic of Armenia in Europe. The Internet by mobile phones is more likely to be used by lower sociodemographic levels and those with lower English skills. It seems that mobile devices may become an alternative route to Internet resources and thus reduce some gaps over time, compared with the traditional PC-based Internet use, with limitations on access, technology, complexity, skill on software, and cost factors. However, they also found that mobile-based users, who do not engage in as much potentially skill-enhancing technology and literacy activities, may not be likely to gain as many economic, material, or cultural benefits from the Internet. The difference may be due to the usability of a small mobile screen, the cost of access via mobile devices, less frequent use, possible shorter usage duration, and the general purpose for the use of two different devices. These hinted that the emphasis of the deficiency is on the investment of technology infrastructure (access issues). Policy makers and local stakeholders should pay more attention to the libraries' role in literacy training even with the expansion of mobile access in American families.

CONCLUSION

This chapter focused on bridging the digital divide in the United States through libraries' Internet access as well as their training on technologies and literacy. There are still many people in the United States who don't have Internet access and who rely on public computers in libraries to fulfill their daily information needs. Libraries also provide various valuable training programs, including e-government services, to bridge the digital gap. Some, particularly within the United States, debate that the digital divide will eventually disappear when economic development reaches a certain level. However, broadband Internet access is becoming a new kind of digital divide between affluent regions and rural and remote areas. When there is a gap, the people with the most resources (status, cognition, education, income, access) are able to be the first to adopt the innovations that are used to then gain more skills; they tend to use additional and different activities more effectively in the early stages.

Rural and underserved populations will be marginalized if this new kind of digital divide broadens. Some rural libraries find themselves in disadvantaged positions due to lower population density and slower broadband coverage, and they might also need more dedicated space for public access and training, which will be discussed in chapter 9.

REFERENCES

Baker, S. (2015). Libraries help close the digital divide. *Washington Post*. Available at http://www.washingtonpost.com/opinions/libraries-help-close-the-digital-divide/2015/05/01/bd6d6e84-edef-11e4-8abc-d6aa3bad79dd_story.html

Becker, S., Crandall, M. D., Fisher, K. E., Blakewood, R., Kinney, B., & Russell-Sauvé, C. (2011). *Opportunity for all: How library policies and practices impact public Internet access* (IMLS-2011-RES-01). Washington, DC: Institute of Museum and Library Services. Available at http://www.imls.gov/assets/1/AssetManager/OppForAll2.pdf

Bertot, J. C., Jaeger, P. T., Lee, J., Debbels, K., McDermott, A. J., & Real, B. (2014). *2013 digital inclusion survey: Survey findings and results.* College Park, MD: Information Policy & Access Center, University of Maryland College Park. Available at http://digitalinclusion.umd.edu/sites/default/files/uploads/2013DigitalInclusionNationalReport.pdf

Council of Economic Advisers. (2015). *Mapping the digital divide.* Washington, DC: Executive Office of the President of the United States. Available at https://www.whitehouse.gov/sites/default/files/wh_digital_divide_issue_brief.pdf

Delaney, M. (2014). How rural and suburban libraries bridge the digital divide [Web log post]. *StateTech Magazine.* Available at http://www.statetechmagazine.com/article/2014/09/city-vs-country

D'Elia, G., Jörgensen, C., Woelfel, J., & Rodger, E. (2002). The impact of the Internet on public library use: An analysis of the current consumer market for library and Internet services. *Journal of American Society for Information Science and Technology, 53*(10), 802–820.

Eisenstein, E. L. (1979). *The printing press as an agent of change: Communications and cultural transformations in early-modern Europe.* Cambridge, United Kingdom: Cambridge University Press.

File, T., & Ryan, C. (2014). *Computer and Internet use in the United States: 2013 American community survey report* (Report no. ACS-28). Washington, DC: United States Census Bureau. Available at http://www.census.gov/history/pdf/2013computeruse.pdf

Institute of Museum and Library Services. (2004). *Toward equality of access: The role of public libraries in addressing the digital divide.* Washington, DC: Institute of Museum and Library Services. Available at http://www.imls.gov/assets/1/AssetManager/Equality.pdf

James, C. (2009). *Young people, ethics, and the new digital media: A synthesis from the GoodPlay project.* Boston, MA: MIT Press.

Kinney, B. (2010). The Internet, public libraries, and the digital divide. *Public Library Quarterly, 29,* 104–161.

Kruger, L. G., & Gilroy, A. A. (2013). *Broadband Internet access and the digital divide: Federal assistance programs.* Washington, DC: Congressional Research Service. Available at https://www.fas.org/sgp/crs/misc/RL30719.pdf

McClure, C., & Jaeger, P. T. (2009). *Public libraries and Internet service roles.* Chicago, IL: ALA.

Merton, R. K. (1968). The Matthew effect in science. *Science, 159*(3810), 56–63.

Newman, R. (2010). How Netflix (and Blockbuster) killed Blockbuster [Web log post]. *U.S. News & World Report.* Available at http://money.usnews.com/money/blogs/flowchart/2010/09/23/how-netflix-and-blockbuster-killed-blockbuster

Pearce, K. E., & Rice, R. E. (2013). Digital divides from access to activities: Comparing mobile and personal computer Internet users. *Journal of Communication, 63,* 721–744.

Plumb, T. K. (2007). Challenges and opportunities for electronic resources (ER) librarians in facing down the digital divide. *Collection Management, 32*(3/4), 327–349.

Rainie, L., & Cohn, D. (2014). *Census: Computer ownership, Internet connection varies widely across U.S.* Washington, DC: Pew Research Center. Available at http://www.pewresearch.org/fact-tank/2014/09/19/census-computer-ownership -internet-connection-varies-widely-across-u-s/

Rodger, E. J., D'Elia, G., & Jörgensen, C. (2001). The public library and the Internet: Is peaceful coexistence possible? *American Libraries, 32*(5), 58–61.

Rogers, E. M. (2003). *Diffusion of innovations* (5th ed.). New York: Free Press.

Stevenson, S. (2009). Digital divide: A discursive move away for the real inequities. *The Information Society, 25,* 1–22.

Udland, M. (2015). Netflix stock explodes after earnings [Web log post]. *Business Insider.* Available at http://www.businessinsider.com/netflix-second-quarter-earnings-2015-7

United Nations. (2006). *Benchmarking e-government: A global perspective.* New York: United Nations. Available at: https://publicadministration.un.org/egovkb/Portals /egovkb/Documents/un/English.pdf

Vavrek, B. (2000). Downsizing the public library. *Public Library Quarterly, 18*(1), 31–34.

Visser, M. (2012). *Digital literacy definition* [Web log post]. Chicago, IL: American Library Association. Available at: http://connect.ala.org/node/181197

Warf, B. (2012). Contemporary digital divides in the United States. *Tijdschrift voor Economische en Sociale Geografie, 104*(1), 1–17.

Warschauer, M. (2003). *Technology and social inclusion: Rethinking the digital divide.* Cambridge, MA: MIT Press.

Zickuhr, K., Raine, L., & Purcell, K. (2013). *Library services in digital age.* Washington, DC: Pew Research Center. Available at http://libraries.pewinternet.org/2013/01/22 /part-4-what-people-want-from-their-libraries/

CHAPTER NINE

Reenvisioning Library Spaces

Traditionally, libraries focused on using physical space to store collections and provide seating for users, along with areas for circulation and technical services. Over the years, it became popular to carve out specific areas for children, teens, adults, and special collections. A later innovation was to have public access computers, computer labs, and business centers. It is critical that small libraries continue to re-envision their spaces to meet current user needs. Changing user needs may require repurposing existing library spaces to reflect demands for new services.

Both physical and virtual library spaces are addressed in this chapter. New trends such as the maker movement and makerspaces in public libraries are also discussed. The chapter also includes what statistics are needed to plan for library space use and the demand of spaces for new technologies. At all times, the limited space available in small libraries is the focus.

PHYSICAL SPACES CONSIDERATIONS

Indoor Physical Space

Library indoor space is limited by the actual dimensions of the building. It is difficult to decide what to include and exclude. Most libraries are going to need a space for their collection, circulation, and operations (technical services, offices, restrooms, and mechanical or utility rooms). Public access computers, computer labs, business centers, conference rooms, and social spaces are all desired. A library might also want to have a coffee shop, bookstore, or other area such as a lounge with vending machines. Many rural and small libraries do not have enough space to accommodate all these needs and desires. To explore ways to rearrange existing space, one can utilize space designing tools.

Space design does not have to be expensive if the librarian chooses free or inexpensive tools. Rippel (2013) demonstrated ShelfShuffler (http://db.tt /O6vXtB9V), a free software package in Microsoft Excel that creates 2-D layouts of furniture, bookshelves, and other library spaces. He also provided detailed steps with examples on using this software.

Three-dimensional design might better represent the space and be easier to visualize. While Auto CAD design software is one of most popular among engineers, it is expensive. There are alternative, inexpensive tools for amateur designers. The software 3Dream (https://www.3dream.net/) is an online 3-D tool for interior design that may be used for space planning. This free online tool allows anyone to build a room using 2-D and 3-D objects from the software. Skold (2012) suggested the study of aesthetics of physical and virtual spaces can be an especially rewarding area to explore in future research.

Collections

One way to free up physical space is to reduce the size of library collections. By managing the size and growth of the print collection through weeding and moving collections online, especially the reference collection that is now almost all available online, libraries may open extra spaces for the amount and variety of public seating, collaborative spaces, and social programs offered. This attention to the collection possibilities keeps library collections relevant to the public with core information services available.

Evans and Saponaro (2005) introduced the process of weeding or deselection to free up the library space. Weeded materials can be stored in a secondary or remote storage place or sent to a disposal such as a Friends of Libraries book sale, Better World Books (http://www.betterworldbooks.com/), gifts or exchange programs, or even recycling. In *Crew: A Weeding Manual for Modern Libraries*, Larson (2012) provided detailed guidelines on weeding children's books, reference collections, nonprint media, and others. The ALA website has annotated bibliographies on weeding library collections at http:// www.ala.org/tools/libfactsheets/alalibraryfactsheet15.

Weeding can be a long process, and its costs include the library staff's effort and time. However, the results can be significant and can free up spaces from bookshelves.

Financial and Technology Challenges

Small libraries repositioning library spaces can be limited by financial, technical, and security challenges. Branin (2007) outlined some of the challenges of any library space design project. A major challenge is funding. Libraries are ready short of money on rising materials costs, personnel, utilities, and maintenance. This means that redesigning library space may often fall behind other funding priorities. In addition, there is always the impact of changing information technologies on library services and space needs. For example, the library building designed for shelving and storage may not be a good design for users' collaborative learning environment where a Wi-Fi connection may be more important than comfortable seating for the person looking at a magazine.

As mentioned in Chapter 6, local grants and private donations for small libraries usually cannot cover the expenses of daily operations but may be a good funding source for library space projects, especially if the needs are based on technical or security concerns.

Security Consideration

Space design must take into consideration library security. Since many rural and small libraries are often located in one building and managed by one staff member at most times, security is particularly important on this matter. Space design should also consider protecting the library building as well as the occupants, the furniture, and the collections. Security cameras, motion detectors, and door alarms are example of necessary security measures, particularly for rural and small libraries where a lot of time there is only one library staff member working in the building. As shown in the ALA's Library Leadership and Management Association (2010), the security issues include both personnel and property safety. The ALA guidelines addressed issues such as prevention of materials losses, fire and emergency protection, physical barrier and lock and key security, personal access and control, security alarms, and electronics. The guideline particularly requested the security devices in case of danger:

> These individuals and any other staff who may face threats or be subjected to excessive hostility should be protected from harmful situations by using a silent duress/panic alarm. Such an alarm would be hidden under the counter or desk. If a situation occurs, the staff person would only need to discretely press a button to summons help from security, police, or both. (Library Leadership and Management Association, 2010, p. 18)

Carey (2008) commented that many librarians introduced seminar rooms and collaborative spaces that presented additional security concerns. Security cameras can be efficient deterrence devices to enhance library security, but experts also cautioned libraries that security cameras may also threaten user privacy. Randall and Newell (2014) reported qualitative studies on public libraries that installed video surveillance systems to prevent crimes, but these libraries also face a dilemma when there is chance that patrons' records in the format of video footage can be pursued by law enforcement. Randall and Newell recommended that libraries be transparent about their surveillance activities by posting notices, signs, and policies on the retention and destruction of and the procedures for sharing video footage. A bibliography on library safety and security can be found here (http://www.ala.org/tools/safety-and-security).

Issues of Children and Teen Spaces

For public libraries or branches that are located near a school, the library often becomes an extension of the classroom and a safe haven for students after school hours. In many public libraries students walk to the library to study or hang out with friends after school hours. Parents who work and are not able to pick up students immediately after school closes often present a challenge. Some librarians have dedicated a space for schoolchildren to read, do research and homework, play games, or simply socialize. Librarians turn this part of the library into a space for school students. In some libraries tutors are available to help students use their time as an extension of the classroom. It can become a place in which students engage in a collaborative learning process, a place where they can develop or refine their critical thinking.

ALA Young Adult Library Service Association (YALSA) published a toolkit called *National Teen Space Guidelines* (2012). The guideline emphasizes that the library environment should encourage the emotional, social, and intellectual development of teens and enhance their sense of belonging, community involvement, and library appreciation. Library teen space should also provide furniture and technologies where users can practice computer skills, such as Internet searching.

There are certain scenarios where the library has to restrict access to the Internet to underage users. ALA published the Internet use policy guideline and excluded access to obscene materials and child pornography, which are not protected by the First Amendment. These are considered "harmful to minors" (http://www.ala.org/bbooks/challengedmaterials/preparation/guidelines-internet-use-policy). Public libraries have to have Internet firewalls to censor some information to children. For example, library policies unusually restrict children and young adults from using the Internet without a consent from a parent or guardian (McKechnie, 1999). Readers, particularly many adult citizens, might prefer a quiet reading space in libraries. At the same time, some young as well adult users may prefer learning commons and gaming space for formal and informal learning, and they hope to have an extended library Web space to access materials from Internet, participate in online discussions, and be more receptive to libraries' social networking sites.

Farkas (2014, p. 26) disagreed with the idea that games are more diversions than they are learning tools; on the contrary, she suggested that gaming "has become an activity that transcends gender, culture, and age" and "can motivate people and make learning more immersive." Once her library changed a library orientation tour to an information scavenger hunt, it attracted many interested users. Virtual rewards such as virtual badges or levels of playing make one's achievement and learning visible and help to transfer the pursuit of achievement to various learning activates.

Many libraries have gaming facilities, such as Xbox, Nintendo WII, and computer stations dedicated to online games. ALA, in partnership with Nordic Games Day and the Australian Library and Information Association, sponsors an annual International Games Day (igd.ala.org), an initiative run by volunteers and libraries around the world. According to ALA website, more than one thousand libraries around the world would demonstrate gaming programs and services in their communities in 2015 (http://igd.ala.org/about/). The activity called e-Sports is a kind of first-person competitive survival online game that has gained a fair amount of media attention in recent years. All these gaming programs and spaces can provide users and teens a place to learn digital literacy skills while hanging out with friends and socializing in a safe environment.

Outdoor Physical Space

Gisolfi (2012) commented that when a new library is planned, the building is placed in an existing landscape, and it is hoped that both the building and the landscape are enhanced. For buildings in city environment, a garden or courtyard may provide the library with quietness and serenity. The suburban environment will have the opportunity to see more open and greener landscapes, while the rural area may see libraries in open landscapes. For functioning purposes, open spaces surrounding the library can be used to organize events for community gathering. For example, a small library in Ontario, California, has a gazebo in its side yard, and this is a popular space rented by couples for Sunday weddings when the library is closed. Receptions must move away from the library, but the gazebo is a very sought after space, and weddings must keep to a very strict schedule to accommodate the numbers who want to get married there.

Conducting Library Space Usage Studies

To plan for redesign or reallocation of spaces in a library, the librarians must conduct a study of space usage. Librarians can use gate counts to determine the number of bodies that come into the library and at what hours. User attendance can also be mapped in detailed floor maps. Pierard and Lee (2011) recommended using a photo observation and photo diaries to capture space characteristics and use of space. Researchers who are assigned this task first watch individuals engage in activities in a natural setting and then take notes on what is observed. They will identify various time periods during the day and evening and take pictures of the same space for a period of days (for example, one week). The photos can be taken by multiple persons to ensure objectivity. All these photos provide insights into a particular space and its use. Photos then can be compared with different time frames, and the story of usage in a time series appears. Photos can also be used to collect feedback from users and library staff.

Another method of studying usage design is to use flipchart to collect feedback directly from users. The free text input from users can then be entered in software and demonstrated as text cloud presentation. Furthermore, librarians can also design library building use surveys and collect data faster, more objectively, and scientifically. Survey data can be quickly compiled, analyzed, and reported using standard statistics software. The opinions from the surveys can be used to make decisions on space arrangement, but it has to be interpreted within the context of real situations. Was the sample size big enough? Did the sample represent the composition of the library's user population? Were survey questions representative of the ideas the librarians wanted to ask? Chapter 10 discusses data collection and analysis techniques, but librarians must interpret their survey results independently and carefully to better serve the community.

Another space-related topic is makerspaces. Makerspaces is a movement to provide a collaborative creation space in the library. To accommodate providing a makerspace, the library must evaluate its existing space and determine ways to arrange or repurpose areas to accommodate this new trend.

MAKERSPACES

A makerspace is a place where people come together to design and build projects. In the past, learning commons, the shared spaces in libraries, were developed to allow users to use information technology, create digital content, collaborate, meet, or study. David Loertscher and Carol Koechlin have compiled data on library learning commons (http://www.schoollearningcommons.info/). Learning commons are typically promoted in academic and school libraries. One of the more recent developments in public libraries is the need to re-envision their space usage, also known as the makerspace movement. This section will discuss the maker movement, followed by information resources and tools on building makerspaces.

Maker Movement

Makerspaces are sometimes referred to as "fablabs," hackerspaces, or tech shops that can make small-scale digital fabrications, and they often provide 3-D printing services to community users (Pryor, 2014). Conceptually, a makerspace is a learning space that is multidimensional and integrated in nature. Another aspect of makerspaces is virtual learning spaces. A virtual learning space can be defined as an online learning environment that complements face-to-face learning and teaching experiences in educational settings (Keppell, Souter, & Riddle, 2011, p. 17). Makerspaces typically "provide access to materials, tools, and technologies to allow for hands-on exploration and participatory learning" (Fisher, 2012, p. 1).

Makerspaces are places to promote community engagement. They are the places to create, build, and share. They allow children and young users to make Lego robots, digital music, movies, and games with computers and mixers. They allow residents to create prototypes for small business products with laser cutters and 3-D printers (American Libraries, 2013).

Information Resources on Building Makerspaces

There are several models of makerspaces that currently are successful in libraries. The first model is the makerspace as a collaborative project with community partners. Since there are for-profit companies that provide technology instructions, tools, and community workshop spaces, small libraries can utilize such existing facilities as community partners and quickly start their joint programs (American Libraries, 2013; Cavalcanti, 2013). Another model is the centralized model, where a library's makerspace is the center of learning and where technology training is provided to community users. This one requires the library staff to train customers in technologies. The last model is to run makerspace as an entrepreneurial project, where the purpose is to develop prototyping for community users and, it is hoped, help the startup small business.

Kroski (2013) compiled a website with articles, blog posts, events, and directories on makerspaces (http://oedb.org/ilibrarian/a-librarians-guide-to-makerspaces/). YALSA (2014) compiled a makerspace toolkit for libraries that can help libraries with planning, partnering, promoting, and evaluating the programs. The toolkit also lists sample maker programs (http://www.ala.org/yalsa/sites/ala.org.yalsa/files/content/MakingintheLibraryToolkit2014.pdf). Based on his survey of 109 libraries, Burke (2014) found the most popular activities in public makerspaces are computer workstations (67%), 3-D printing (46%), photo editing (45%), video editing (45%), computer programming (43%), art and crafts (37%), scanning photos (36%), website creation (34%), digital music recording (33%), 3-D modeling (31%), Arduino or Raspberry Pi (30%), and other activities (p. 6). She also listed resources for makerspace ideas, such as audio, image, and video production; crafts and artistic creation; electronic and robotics; 3-D printing and prototyping; and so on.

The Value of Makerspaces to Library Services

Regardless of the former titles that are assigned to them, makerspaces are becoming important outreach tools to community users. "Libraries are able to adopt new approaches and use incredible creativity in engaging community members in new ways, becoming fertile spaces for making activities," says Susan Hildreth, director of IMLS (as cited by Britton, 2012). Loertscher (2012) suggested that makerspaces are similar to "learning commons" that allow students to work collaboratively in libraries, but there is more potential for "family gatherings" and other outreach activities. According to Kurti, Kurti, and Fleming (2014), makerspaces are learner driven, allowing learners to personalize their experiences using inquiry-based approaches to develop their knowledge. Yet librarians must understand how to navigate community cultures in order to collaborate and inspire experimentation, tinkering, and creation within a makerspace. Hence, community engagement coupled with space and tools are crucial elements for makerspaces.

Makerspaces are a means to demonstrate the value of libraries to social leaders, elected officials, and resource allocators. They are a vital part of communities because they have the power to democratize access to information and tools that individuals would normally not be able to use (O'Duinn, 2014). Makerspaces can be tool to encourage community users to enhance individual skills and interests in science, technology, engineering, and mathematics (STEM).

There are great divisions in access to STEM resources associated with socioeconomic, gender, and ethnic lines (National Math + Science Initiative, 2014). O'Duinn (2014) asserts that makerspaces can counteract these disparities by introducing communities to scientific inquiry that reflects the interests of community members. This allows community members to become citizen scientists who endeavor to find solutions that are relevant to their needs.

Makerspace activities do not have to be limited to a particular age group. They are healthy for all ages. In particular, they are beneficial to youth who need to understand the inquiry process. A common misconception is that it is okay to wait until youth reach middle school or high school to teach them technology literacy skills. Nonetheless, students need to learn these skills at a young age so that they will be proficient when they matriculate throughout K–12 (National Math + Science Initiative, 2014) and enter college (Latham & Gross, 2011). Makerspaces in public libraries offer the opportunity to practice these essential skills in an information environment.

As a center of community and a gathering place, rural and small libraries may eventually experience the transformation from being a book center to becoming a technology hub in their communities. For example, the Southern Prairie Library System, located in Altus Public Library in Altus, Oklahoma, received an IMLS grant on makerspaces in 2015 (http://altustimes.com/top-stories/1057 /library-creating-mobile-makerspaces). The project supports the library system on science, technology, engineering, and math (STEM) materials and activities for arts and crafts design, simple coding and electronics, basic robotics, 3-D printing, and Lego creative building projects.

Makerspaces can be inexpensive and effective, too. IFLA reported ideas of tech and nontech makerspaces (http://www.ifla.org/node/9631), such as handmade jewelry making workshops, creative recycling, MusicLab, and so on. Similar projects have been seen in Wyoming (http://wyomingpublicmedia .org/post/libraries-make-space-3-d-printers-rules-are-sure-follow#stream/0). Social media have abundant recent development on makerspaces in libraries, including a person's blog on Arizona libraries with makerspace or 3-D printing, as well as local makerspaces that may not be affiliated with libraries (https://3dprintinglibrarian.wordpress.com/library-makerspace-directory/). All the examples above demonstrate the use of makerspace and its position in the reallocation of library physical spaces.

Library virtual spaces can include library websites, as well Facebook, Twitter, Instagram, and other social network sites from the libraries, as well the interaction with personal learning spaces.

While rural libraries pay more attention to physical space and buildings, virtual spaces should be paid attention to also, since more and more residents are using library websites and e-books.

It is important to organize the library website so it is easy to navigate and so users can find their way quickly to e-resources. Jasek (2004) published a pamphlet regarding library website design and usability issues. It covers consistency, orientation, page layout, aesthetics, graphics, flexibility and efficiency of use, accessibility, usability testing, and so on. The resource is online at http://digital.csic.es/bitstream/10261/2926/1/howtodesign[1].pdf.

To build engaging content for libraries, small libraries may not have the expertise to build Web presences through social networking sites, but certainly they can learn from best practices implemented by bigger libraries. Harmon and Messina (2013) compiled best practices from major public libraries such as the blogging activities from the Missouri River Regional Library (p. 2), the Facebook campaign from the Farmington Public Library (p. 56), and the Twitter account of the Vancouver Public Library (p. 65). All these provide examples on how successful library virtual spaces are built and maintained, regardless of what devices are used to visit library virtual spaces.

Buerkett (2014) urged libraries to create a virtual library space since many users have mobile devices and expect to access information 24–7. She also recommended extending the library virtual space from the OPAC and placing the most important resources on the webpage, for example, links to research materials such as pathfinders, databases, online catalogs, and schedule calendars, as well as games, downloadable e-books and audiobooks, and so on.

SOCIAL AND CULTURAL SPACE IN LIBRARY SERVICES

Libraries are traditionally a place where local residents meet, learn, socialize, do business, and participate in their children's programs. A Pew Research report (Zickuhr, Rainie, & Purcell, 2013) found that the library as a community space continue to be an important function of libraries in today's digital-enhanced environments. The same report also revealed that "a warm, welcoming and friendly space is hard to find these days, and the public library has the remarkable opportunity to become a community gathering place in communities where such a space is sorely missing," commented by one of their panelists of library staff members (p. 67).

Even with the potential and unique advantage of providing access to books, online resources, and Internet access, libraries may not take it for granted that they are the only place in town that people can gather. Bookstores these days allow people to browse and reading books, and many coffee shops have a more inviting environment with free public Wi-Fi. The continuing threat of budget cut from city and state funding agencies, plus the convenience of home and mobile-based Internet, leaves libraries in the vulnerable position of reduced foot traffic and perceived irrelevance in a digital society (Scott, 2012).

Social networking is becoming part of life and a communication channel for 74% of the U.S. online population. According to another Pew Research (2014) report, 71% of the U.S. online population use Facebook, and 23% of online adults use Twitter; 26% of them use Instagram, 28% use Pinterest, and 28% use LinkedIn (http://www.pewinternet.org/fact-sheets/social-networking -fact-sheet/). It is noteworthy that 90% of the population aged 18–29 use social networking sites, and even 56% of online adults aged 65 and older do. This report also found that average Facebook users receive more information from their friends than contribute to their friends, because there exists a type of "power user," who specializes in various activities and likes to make contributions to their social groups.

Now libraries have direct, free communication access to potentially 71% of the online population in their communities via social media. Social media sites should be treated as personalized virtual spaces that a library can provide information on organizational profiles, videos, blogs, posted events, and more important, contact friends, particularly those "power users" of Facebook or Twitter who can be advocates for library services and events. Library staff members who maintain library virtual spaces are making the same effort as face-to-face librarians when they greet new users; post events; promote upcoming new books, movies, and music; and maintain good user relations in the communities. Some libraries post community surveys and have open dialogue with community users to seek their opinions on various aspects of decision making for the library. This will give community users a sense of ownership and feel an inviting environment of the library. It is beneficial to collaborate with other libraries or community organizations to mutually promote events that can draw the attention of more potential users. In addition, power users, when they help to promote libraries in social media, can be extreme valuable and fast and can reach out to a broad user base. Social media are becoming more and more powerful tools to shape and influence policies and politics. They become sources of political news, shape the political movement, and connect voters. Libraries as virtual spaces should maintain their natural position and allow all citizens to express ideas freely, the same as libraries will allow in physical buildings.

CONCLUSION

This chapter envisions library physical and virtual space design, with an emphasis on library physical space considerations and library makerspaces. As the nation's economy moves from manufacturing to creative, financial, educational, and health services, libraries should fully embrace the idea of being places where community users not only acquire new information but also become producers of knowledge as well as creators of digital and physical content (Imholz, 2008). All these recent ideas make library space design a comprehensive planning process that should consider physical, virtual, social network, Web, and even outdoor spaces.

At the same time, it is very critical for rural libraries to seek partnership with the city, volunteers, and other organizations in the community to bring experts together in the library to help patrons plan and implement space-related projects, since many rural and small libraries have limited staff. User needs and benefits to library user services should be assessed before any space projects are designed and implemented.

REFERENCES

American Libraries. (2013). Manufacturing makerspaces. *American Libraries*. Available at http://americanlibrariesmagazine.org/2013/02/06/manufacturing-makerspaces/

Branin, J. (2007). Shaping our space: Envisioning the new research library. *Journal of Library Administration, 46*(2), 27–54.

Britton, L. (2012). The making of maker spaces, Part 1: Space for creation, not just consumption [Web log post]. *Library Journal*. Available at http://www.thedigitalshift.com/2012/10/public-services/the-makings-of-maker-spaces-part-1-space-for-creation-not-just-consumption/

Buerkett, R. (2014). Where to start? Creating virtual library spaces. *Knowledge Quest, 42*(4), 23–27.

Burke, J. J. (2014). *Makerspaces: A practical guide for librarians*. Lanham, MD: Rowman & Littlefield.

Carey, J. (2008). Library security by design. *Library & Archive Security, 21*(2), 129–140.

Cavalcanti, G. (2013). Making makerspaces: Creating a business model [Web log post]. *Make*. http://makezine.com/2013/06/04/making-makerspaces-creating-a-business-model/

Evans, G. E., & Saponaro, M. Z. (2005). *Developing library and information center collections*. Santa Barbara, CA: Libraries Unlimited.

Farkas, M. (2014). Just a game? *American Libraries, 45*(1/2), 26.

Fisher, E. (2012). Makerspaces move into academic libraries [Web log post]. *ACRL TechConnect*. Retrieved from http://acrl.ala.org/techconnect/?p=2340

Gisolfi, P. (2012). Libraries and their landscapes. *Library Journal, 137*(20), 38–41. Available at http://lj.libraryjournal.com/2012/12/buildings/libraries-and-their-landscapes-feature/#_

Harmon, C., & Messina, M. (2013). *Using social media in libraries: Best practices*. Lanham, MD: Scarecrow Press.

Jasek, C. (2004). *How to design library websites to maximize usability* (pamphlet #5). San Diego, CA: Library Connect Editorial Office. Available at http://digital.csic.es/bitstream/10261/2926/1/howtodesign[1].pdf

Keppell, M., Souter, K., & Riddle, M. (2011). Physical and virtual learning spaces in higher education: Concepts for the modern learning environment. Hershey, NY: IGI Global.

Kurti, R. S., Kurti, D. D., & Fleming, L. I. (2014). The environment and tools of great educational makerspaces. *Teacher Librarian, 42*(1), 8.

Larson, J. (2012). *Crew: A weeding manual for modern libraries.* Austin, TX: Texas State Library and Archives Commission. Available at https://www.tsl.texas.gov /sites/default/files/public/tslac/ld/ld/pubs/crew/crewmethod12.pdf

Library Leadership and Management Association. (2010). *Library security guidelines document.* Chicago, IL: American Library Association. Available at http://www.ala .org/llama/sites/ala.org.llama/files/content/publications/LibrarySecurityGuide.pdf

Loertscher, D. V. (2012). Maker spaces and the learning commons. *Teacher Librarian, 9*(6), 45–46.

McKechnie, L. (E.F.). (2001). Children's access to services in Canadian public libraries. *The Canadian Journal of Information and Library Science, 26*(4), 37–55.

O'Duinn, F. (2014). Science by people: Public librarians meet citizen scientists. *Feliciter, 60*(1). Available at http://www.cla.ca/feliciter/2014/1/mobile/#oduinn

Pierard, C., & Lee, N. (2011). Studying space: Improving space planning with user studies. *Journal of Access Services, 8*(4), 190–207.

Pryor, S. (2014). Implementing a 3D printing service in an academic library. *Journal of Library Administration, 54*(1), 1–10.

Randall, D. P., & Newell, B. C. (2014). The panoptic librarian: The role of video surveillance in the modern public library. *iConference 2014 Proceedings.* Available at https://www.ideals.illinois.edu/bitstream/handle/2142/47307/132_ready.pdf

Rippel, C. (2013). *Let's play library with shelf shuffler and collection manager.* Paper presented at 2013 Association for Rural and Small Libraries annual conference. Omaha, NE.

Scott, M. (2012). How libraries and bookstores became the new community centers [Web log post]. *The New Geography.* Available at http://www.newgeography.com /content/002629-how-libraries-and-bookstores-became-new-community-centers

Skold, O. (2012). Effects of virtual space in learning: A literature review. *First Monday, 17*(1/2). Available at http://firstmonday.org/ojs/index.php/fm/article/view/3496/3133

Young Adult Library Service Association. (2012). *National teen space guidelines.* Chicago, IL: American Library Association. Available at http://www.ala.org/yalsa /sites/ala.org.yalsa/files/content/guidelines/guidelines/teenspaces.pdf

Zickuhr, K., Rainie, L., & Purcell, K. (2013). *Library services in the digital age.* Washington, DC: Pew Internet & American Project. Available at http://libraries .pewinternet.org/2013/01/22/part-5-the-present-and-future-of-libraries/

CHAPTER TEN

Assessing User Needs and Improving User Services

Assessing user needs is critical to improving user services. This process requires collecting information from a variety of sources. This chapter will cover collecting available public data from the census and other openly available data, data generated by the library staff, and data from library systems. Social networking data and data from teen services are gathered to determine how to reach this population through social networking. The discussion of user needs analysis includes an environmental scan with information on methods of analyzing community data, with a caution about data security and user privacy. The chapter ends with an evaluation and assessments for compiling library statistics and evaluating collections.

Rural and small library directors often find themselves landing a new job but cannot find any statistics needed in order to immediately compile an annual report or evidence showing that the library is meeting its targeted goals. Many small library directors fear the complexity of data collection and analysis. For librarians to make sure that their libraries, as an organizational entity, grow in a targeted direction and to ensure that all staff and governing board members work in the same direction, a strategic plan is needed in order to create benchmarks to meet established goals. Creating a strategic plan requires solid data to support the process and assessments, especially data pertaining to the users and services, and this data must be collected before the real planning process can begin. Gathering information about users and services can also be used to gain more political support in the local community, as sharing these results can help to change public perception. The final goal is to present the library and its services as a necessity rather than a nicety in the community, and the assessment tools used to collect the appropriate data are vital in achieving such goal.

This chapter will address how librarians can collect user service information in order to prepare for annual reports, outreach projects, grant proposals, and strategic planning. Openly available data from Census.gov is discussed, followed by generating one's own data for libraries, and finally self-generated data-collection methods are analyzed. This chapter shows the application of theories to practice, and the chapter will focus on data collection, evaluation, and assessment.

COLLECTING PUBLICLY AVAILABLE DATA

An abundance of data is available from public sources. Using this data will both save time and also save from any concerns that local collection of data would have any bias.

Publicly Available Data from Census

Blake, Martin, and Du (2011) stated the importance of collecting "the geographic, demographic, and statistical characteristics of a library's service area along with the role the library has historically and currently plays in it" (p. 12). Some data are openly accessible such as the U.S. Census data, and using this can be a starting point to understand local population, geography, business, and community assets. For example, census data on state and county Quick-Facts allow one to search by a county or city name, and the computer will display people, businesses, and geographic information such as population distributed by age and racial groups, educational level, household income, number of business firms, and land area (http://quickfacts.census.gov/qfd/states/). One can simply browse by state name and then choose from the county or city names listed in the pull-down menu.

Census data from Presidio County, Texas, reveals that 82% of this county consists of Hispanic or Latino speakers, which strengthen the request to support on ESL or literacy training projects (http://quickfacts.census.gov/qfd /states/48/48377.html). Another case is the demographics of the city of Glen Carbon, Illinois, whose library won the 2010 Best Small Library in America award from *Library Journal*. Residents of the city of Glen Carbon have a high level of education, as the percentage of high school graduates or higher is 94.2%, and 49% have college degrees. Both statistics are higher than the state average. As this city has such a high level of education, this might make the city a good candidate for the promotion of noon lunch programming and technology resources such as e-books (http://quickfacts.census.gov/qfd/states/17/1729639. html). Lastly, statistics show Alpine County, California, has a higher percentage of American Indians and Alaska Natives, 23.9% of population, making it a unique location to initiate GED programs (http://quickfacts.census.gov/qfd /states/06/06003.html). Demographics from these counties or cities provide solid data for librarians to develop programs and service ideas.

Data from the U.S. Census (http://www.census.gov) can be the most extensive and rich data that a library can use to understand the community for many types of reports and project proposals. Census data at a state and county level, found through QuickFacts, also covers information regarding population, age, race, housing, income, and languages that one can use to compile a user profile analysis. The University of Michigan Library also compiled a research guide on U.S. Census and demographic information, titled "The American Community Survey." For example, census data are available for downloading into a CSV or Excel file format that can be used directly for statistical reports. The site also provides information on how to generate maps using census data (http://guides.lib.umich.edu/census). Another source to download the bulk census data into a CSV or Excel file is Census.IRE.org (http://census.ire.org/data/bulkdata.html), where one can download data on state and summary levels (county and county subdivision) and in specifics, such as population, race, gender by age, household sizes, and so on. The CSV files can be then used for analysis using Excel or any statistical software.

Other Openly Available Data

Other accessible data include previous library annual reports that might be located through government information portals, in addition to reports prepared by a library for its governing authorities such as city managers, city council, county commissioners, board of trustees, and so on. A library's previous reports may include its history of circulation reports, attendance at various library programs, budgeting, and expenditures. An example of a report at the state level is the Texas Public Library statistics (https://www.tsl.texas.gov/ld/pubs/pls/index.html), where one can download both statewide and local comparison statistics in Excel format. One of such reports is the 2014 statistics from all reporting libraries, where each library's essential data are available, including service population, square footage, expenditures on salaries, benefits, and materials, as well as operating revenues from county, city or school districts, capital revenues from foundation and grants, and so on. The full statistical analysis is available in tabular format at http://www.countingopinions.com/pireports/report.php?e3860e0715c0703ee3f7f661b666446e

Similar state library reports are available online; the State of New York library report (http://www.nysl.nysed.gov/libdev/libs/), Illinois Public Library report (http://www.cyberdriveillinois.com/departments/library/libraries/IPLAR/home.html), New Mexico Public Library report (http://www.nmstatelibrary.org/nm-publiclibrary-annualreport), California Library Statistics Portal (https://www.library.ca.gov/lds/librarystats.html), and Florida Library Data and Statistics (http://dos.myflorida.com/library-archives/services-for-libraries/more-programs/library-data-and-statistics/). Similar reports regarding state library statistics can provide valuable data useful in understanding a library and its user service environment.

Many times librarians need to learn about new trends in a community or need to understand pieces of service information that are not included in census data, previous reports, or the automation systems. When one has exhausted one's use of openly accessible data, one may choose to generate additional data.

LIBRARY-GENERATED SERVICE DATA

Librarians may generate data using several methods including conducting a survey, interviewing, or observing clientele. Librarians may also locate data if they are a member of a library system, and that system collects data.

Survey and Interview Data

Surveys and interviews may seem to be less expensive ways to gather and interpret the opinions of the local people, but remember these may take staff time or require time to train volunteers to conduct the surveys or interviews. They are most powerful in providing a way to confirm or adapt the opinions held by the library managers and staff. Using surveys and interviews allows the library staff to find out what their constituents want rather than simply deciding and implementing what programs and services to offer without statistical support.

The choice between data-collection methods, surveys, interviews, and observations depends on the specific situation. Surveys can be a fast way to collect data from a large number of people, and the results can be quantifiable, while face-to-face or phone interviews can collect lengthy, unrestricted responses (Case, 2012, p. 235). Charbonneau (2007, p. 54) commented that "constructing carefully written questions and a well-designed survey questionnaire can help illuminate the needs and desires of both current and potential library clientele, shape or reshape services, or guide strategic planning decisions."

Connaway and Powell's work (2010, pp. 148–149) is classic reading in the library field, and it covers in detail how to design surveys and interview questions, as well as how to analyze and report data. They define types of questions as factual questions, opinion and attitude questions, information questions, self-perception questions, standards of action questions, questions about actual past or present behavior, and projective questions (Connaway & Powell, 2010; Peterson, 2000; Hernon, 2000).

A factual question is used to ascertain some facts about the respondents. An example would be, "What is your gender?" or "What is your highest level of education?"

An opinion or attitude question is intended to determine a person's ideas, inclination, prejudices, convictions, and so on. They tend to be more subjective than factual questions. An example would be, "How do you feel about the self-checkout kiosk?"

An information question measures respondents' knowledge about some topics, and it might take a longer time for respondents to complete. An example of such a question would be, "What are two pieces of knowledge you learned from this information literacy class?"

A self-perception question is similar to an attitude question, but it is restricted to oneself. For example, "How do you feel about reading a book on a tablet?"

A standard of action concerns how respondents would act in certain circumstances. For example, "Would you use our library more often if we open on Sundays?"

A question about actual past or present behavior tends to be more narrow on behavior, such as the use of information. An example is "How often did you use an e-book reader last month"? This particular question may also fall into the opinion and attitude category.

A projective question seeks a person's answer about their beliefs and attitudes about others. It can be subjective and answers can be weak and should be used in caution. For example, "What would the people in your neighbor feel if we open a new branch in the south side of the city?"

Connaway and Powell's (2010) defined two types of survey questions: open-ended and structured questions. Open-ended questions permit free responses and are not restricted to limited types of answers. For example, "What do you think about our library's new website?"

Structured questions include checklists and scaled response questions. An example of a checklist is "How often did you use the public library in the past 12 months?" with choices such as "Never, 1–5, 6–10, 11–15, 16 or more." Scaled responses use a rating scale on which a respondent selects a numeric score to represent the answer. For example, "Using a scale of 1–5, where 1 means 'least important,' and 5 means 'most important,' rank how important library DVD rental is for your family."

Survey and interview data can provide useful and up-to-date information from the community. It can measure the impact of library services in the community and measure whether a library should continue or discontinue a particular service. Librarians can also use service data from library automation systems, where the data are considered more objective.

Data from Library Automation Systems

When libraries use an automation system, the librarian may be able to use computer-generated data for routine reports as well as in the decision-making process. For example, a library may need to generate a biannual financial report, or to determine which book orders were submitted and completed, or to know the number of interlibrary loan transactions and cost related to lending or the borrowing process. A library may also need to know the most popular books that are checked out recently and what age groups are interested in a particular type of books, so the library can adjust its purchasing orders.

Within the library, the library automation system can generate user information and library visits records, as well as acquisition, cataloging, and circulation data, budget reports, and even Web access logs. These reports can be broken down by annual, monthly, weekly, or daily intervals. Data are created daily in the daily work process and exist objectively out of the library staff's direct intervention. For example, the Koha Library Automation System can generate the following reports under the "Report" function: acquisition statistics, patron statistics, catalog statistics, circulation statistics, serial statistics, hold statistics, patrons with the most checkouts, most circulated items, patrons with no checkouts, items with no checkouts, catalog by item type, lost items, and average loan time.

If a librarian or someone who can provide web support adds a simple JavaScript code into their webpages, they can use Google Analytics to track visitor information. This is an easy way to collect website traffic data and is popularly favored by many libraries. Sheehan used Google Analytics to track and identify new potential users to their libraries (https://lakesuperiorlibrariessym posium.files.wordpress.com/2013/04/discovering_our_patrons_using_ga.pdf)

For small and rural libraries who are able to offer Wi-Fi use in the library, the statistics from this use would be extremely valuable. However, it is another daunting task to assess the library Wi-Fi use. Library Research Service (n.d.) published strategies on how to accurately track and report Wi-Fi usage data, including collecting network logs and scanning and counting network devices. Using Google Analytics, librarians can report the total number of wireless devices that access the website during a year or during a typical week and can exclude wireless use of the library's own equipment.

With appropriate tools and enough time, librarians can collect enough community and library usage data for library annual reports as well as for strategic planning purpose. The next section discusses collecting information about social networking.

Social Networking Data for Libraries

Various librarians nationwide are considered early users of social networking sites, including Facebook, Flickr, Google+, Pinterest, Twitter, Instagram, Yelp, and so on (American Library Association, 2013). Most of the social networking sites are for communication with "friends" and to gain "likes." On the other hand, social media such as YouTube are digital content sharing sites that were created to achieve the most views and at the same time allow registered users to "like" or subscribe to the "channels" that they wish to follow. Many librarians are implementing the technologies that can best advocate their services in order to have the greatest return on the investment of their resources. *American Libraries* (2013) surveyed 471 public libraries to gain insights as to how they market themselves and found 86% of libraries use social media, and the top two social media platforms used by libraries were Facebook (99%) and Twitter (56%). Pinterest is earning its share of market too, with 30% of libraries reporting that they were pinning (Dowd, 2013). Dowd also mentioned that 48% of libraries did not assess the effect of their Facebook posts and that some libraries posted events but not did not generate any user engagement. This is particularly true for one-staff small libraries, where staff time and attention is very precious. Libraries need to have a strong social media team with strategies in place regarding what topics are to be posted to social media and how to attract greater community interest. The data generated from social media should be periodically measured and treated just like radio, local newspapers, and other conventional media in the community, in order to more accurately assess its impact.

Success within social media is often be measurable. For example, in 2010, the Central Rappahannock Regional Library in Fredericksburg, Virginia, made a morale-boosting YouTube video for a staff appreciation function, titled "Libraries Will Survive," and it attracted 13,000 views in its first week; as of today (June 2015) the combined short and long versions have 208,000 views. The video spread through Facebook, via bloggers and news outlets, and created both national and international fans. The video communicated one simple message to viewers: "when the economy is tough, people need their libraries more" (Dankowski, 2013).

An excellent service to offer from small and rural libraries is the one for children and teens, because earlier in the book it was noted that the people who do not always see the need to support libraries, perhaps, are teens. If one is going to reach teens, the subject of the next section, social media can be an excellent way to do this.

Libraries and Teens

The most important user group for libraries to reach out to through social networking and technology is teens. The ALA 2013 library report noted that teens are on the forefront of adopting new technologies and that this user group generates the greatest amount of digital social activity including texting, chatting, tweeting, linking, and so on. They are the incoming lifelong generation of libraries. "If libraries are not effectively serving teens, they are not only failing to reach an important segment of their local population, but missing opportunities to help teens become lifelong users of libraries" (American Libraries, 2013, p. 41). Teens are digital natives and heavy users of mobile technologies and gaming users, as well as digital content producers and consumers.

Libraries also have rich data to use as a demonstration of their impact through the employment of Twitter, Facebook, Pinterest, and Instagram, and there are abundant cases of how libraries can use this data on text analysis. The next section discusses user needs analysis.

USER NEEDS ANALYSIS

After collecting data related to the community, librarians can strategically analyze the user needs under three areas: from a higher level of library environmental analysis to a smaller scale on community data analysis and, finally, down to individual user needs, particularly data security and privacy concerns.

Library Environmental Analysis

Morrison (1992) defined the term environmental scanning from the business perspective, as a method "that enables decision makers both to understand the external environment and the interconnections of its various sectors and to translate this understanding into the institution's planning and decision-making processes" (p. 86). Morrison further defined three levels of environmental scanning: the first level is task environment, the second level is industry environment, and the third level is macroenvironment scanning. The task environment reports the institution's set of customers. This set of customers, when in a rural and small library environment, is unique, depending on the local social-economical settings; these customers include community users, the board of trustees, and the friends of the libraries, if available. The second level is the industry environment, or all enterprises associated with an organization. In a small city this includes all businesses related to a library. The last level, macroenvironment, means changes in the "social, technical, economic, environmental, and political (STEEP) sections" affecting the library, such as a state-level budget cut that can impact many libraries (p. 88).

Librarians (Downing, Brown, & Colletti, n.d.) defined an environment as "the surroundings, conditions, circumstances and influences affecting the development of a library community, group, organization, etc.," and an environmental scan is "the careful monitoring of an organization's internal and external environments for detecting early signs of opportunities and threats that may influence its current and future plans. In comparison, surveillance is confined to a specific objective or a narrow sector."

An environmental analysis can be completed by doing a SWOT analysis, a tool useful for understanding an organization's strength and weakness, and identifying both the opportunities and the threats a library faces. It involves a "formalized examination of the Strength and Weakness that are internal to the organization as well as the Opportunity and Threats that are factors not specifically under the control of the organization but important to the future of information and knowledge services" (Stueart & Moran, 2007, p. 102).

Manktelow (n.d.) listed detailed steps of doing a SWOT analysis on his website (mindtools.com). Since this toolkit is particularly useful for individuals without a business marketing background, it fits rural and small library managers well, since many of them are the only staff member, or with very few helpers, working in a library setting. The toolkit has very good questions on strengths that fit rural and small libraries, such as "what advantages does your organization have," "what do you do better than anyone else," and "what unique or lowest-cost resources can you draw upon that others can't." Ideas on opportunities and interesting trends that are related to libraries can include changes in technologies, government policy in the community, and changes in social patterns, population profiles, and lifestyle changes.

Community Data and Analytic Methods

User needs analysis should describe the community and where a library is located. Community data can include geographic, demographic, and statistical characteristics of the service area, along with historical and current roles that the library plays. If the community is in a farming area where migrant workers are employed, they may be a group that does not use the library at all or seldom uses its services. For a community that is located near a metropolitan area where residents commute to work outside their community, these residents may be a potentially underserved population for the library. These community features such as miles to the nearest town, airports, and nearby hospitals are important to describe the community profile (Blake, Martin, & Du, 2011).

To analyze the community data, there are several tools available to visualize data from the U.S. Census. For example, Social Explorer is an online demographic research tool that lets "users create maps and reports to illustrate, analyze, and understand demography and social change" (Social Explorer, n.d., http://www.socialexplorer.com/about). Social Explorer can create interactive and easily navigable maps that users can utilize in order to understand the vast array of available demographic information. The output is a professional-looking map that can be used directly in professional-looking reports, presentations, or graphical reports.

Another important source to acquire community demographic data is the American Fact Finder (http://factfinder.census.gov/faces/nav/jsf/pages /index.xhtml). This online tool enables users to search popular facts and frequently requested data about a community. Examples of popular facts include population, age, prevalent businesses and industries, education, governments, housing, income, origins, languages spoken, poverty levels, race, and even the number of residing veterans. There is step-by-step guided search over census information. In addition, one can go to the download center (http://factfinder. census.gov/faces/nav/jsf/pages/download_center.xhtml) to choose various datasets to download as CSV file for Microsoft Excel or any statistical analysis software.

Data Security and Data Privacy Issues

Data security and user privacy are two aspects. The first, data security for library data, concerns the keeping of data collected from the sources discussed in this chapter. A small library would be devastated if library data were lost and backups were not available. For libraries that contract their automation services to vendors, data security is dependent on the vendor, and in turn, the librarians have fewer concerns regarding data backups and system operations. Many small to medium sized libraries use open source library automation, and data backup and security issues are the responsibility of the library staff.

In addition, data security is more than the integrity of the library automation systems, but the library hardware and software security are two of the greatest the concerns as they relate to user information. In addition to virus and spyware issues, when users browse the Internet, they may download music, videos, or illegitimate digital content and their actions will count as copyright infringements on the library's network.

Another important issue is for librarians to teach community users, particularly teens, about privacy and security issues over the Internet and social networking sites. Internet browsers, for example, Google Chrome and Safari, tend to save a user's login and password information after a pop-up prompt. It is often seen that careless people leave their e-mail accounts open on public computers, and their private information becomes available for other people to access.

Barnes (2006) warned that teenagers often freely give up personal information in order to join social networks on the Internet and afterward are surprised when their parents or teachers read their journals. Even worse, some younger children fake their age and register for social networking sites even though they are not at the required age (13 years is the common age minimum for creating account), and the personal information revealed by teenagers on these sites have the potential to attract sexual predators. Communities can be outraged by the personal information posted by young people online. Libraries have the responsibility to safeguard user privacy when providing various online services.

Agosto and Abbas (2011) suggested that many libraries have successfully entered the world of online social networking through posting information about new book and media purchases, advertising library programs and events, and providing reference and reader's advisories via the sites' instant messaging (IM) or e-mail services. They commented:

> Libraries need to keep in mind that privacy and security are important issues to consider in designing and delivering online library services for young adults. Teens (and adults) might think of social network as private spaces, but they are not truly private. Frequent articles in the popular press indicate that many adults worry issues of information privacy and information security when it comes to online interactions and to posting information online, particularly in social networking environments. (p. 60)

ALA Young Adult Library Services Association (YALSA) (2011) also published a toolkit for libraries to educate the community and teens about social media. Particularly, they recommend sessions with teens on safety and privacy concerns and recommend training teens to decide whether or not digital photos should be kept private or open to the public.

EVALUATION AND ASSESSMENT METHODS

To demonstrate their community impact, rural libraries often need to understand the usage of basic evaluation and assessment methods. This section will introduce compiling library statistics, followed by conducting the evaluation of library collection.

Compiling Library Statistics

Libraries need to provide data regarding annual operation for local and institutional reports, as well as accreditation purposes for a variety of reasons. In most states, librarians need to report not just to their local funding bodies but also to their state libraries. In Texas, for example, all public libraries submit an annual report to the Texas State Library and Archives Commission (TSLAC) (https:// www.tsl.texas.gov/ld/pubs/arsma/index.html). The libraries are required to report the following areas: library information, public service outlets (branches, bookmobiles, expansions, etc.), expenditures, local financial efforts or funding support, and revenues. The TSLAC website also linked a worksheet to complete an annual report for the current fiscal year (https://www.tsl.texas.gov/sites /default/files/public/tslac/ld/pubs/arsma/2014ARWorksheet-Complete2.pdf). All reports are then processed and are downloadable for research and comparison.

Many rural librarians find compiling statistics for reports to be a daunting task. If one is employed as a new library director without a mentor, it will be overwhelming to compile the needed statistics and prepare for the annual report. In addition to library statistical reports, occasionally a library needs to evaluate their user services for community outreach planning, strategic planning, and community user needs assessment. A first source to get help could be a librarian in a nearby library. Next, consultants in the state library are available to offer help. If a librarian is reluctant to ask either of those individuals, continuing educational courses from places like WebJunction can help librarians to overcome the technical difficulties with no or minimum cost (Eggett, 2014). WebJunction's continuing education courses are supported by OCLC, the Gates Foundation, and many state library agencies across the United States (http:// www.webjunction.org/events/webjunction/library-surveys-for-success.html)

Survey data may show that library users are satisfied with inadequate or irrelevant library collections. Size of the collections is not relevant if most the collection should be weeded. If a small library has limited budget, they cannot always afford the cost related to interlibrary loan. Evaluating library collection is an important step from the standpoint of demonstrating that extra funds are necessary to replace an out-of-date collection. The next section will address some general guidelines for evaluating library collections.

Evaluation of Library Collections

A new library director may inherit a library with collections that have been neglected for a long time, and before the librarians can weed the collections, the librarian might be required to first assess the collections. Collection analysis is a systematic process for determining the quality of the library's collection. There is abundant information on library collection analysis, including an ALA webpage on standards and guidelines on collection development (http://www .ala.org/tools/guidelines/standardsguidelines#CollectionDvmt).

Larson (2008) emphasized that collections should be created, developed, and maintained to meet the needs of the community they serve. An overview for completing a collection analysis and included links for evaluation and additional resources is provided. One of the links is OCLC's collection analysis service (http://www.oclc.org/collectionanalysis/default.htm).

Size, currency, turnover rates, and other statistical factors can indicate the quality of the collection. She commented:

> The central concept in the process of analyzing a collection is that collections are created, developed, and maintained to meet the needs of the community they serve. This means that the collection must remain relevant and useful to the people who are using it. Therefore, collection evaluation must also include an analysis of how well the materials are currently meeting needs and how likely the materials (and the collection) are to continue meeting the needs of current and future users. (Larson, 2008, p. 1)

Larson (2012) suggested a collection evaluation method CREW (Continuous Review, Evaluation, and Weeding) and listed detailed steps on children's materials, reference collection, nonprint media, e-books, and even computers. The collection evaluation guidelines include to weed the collection in a "MUSTIE" condition, which means misleading (inaccurate), ugly (worn or beyond repair), superseded (by new editions), trivial (of no discernible literary or scientific merit), irrelevant (to the community), and can be found at elsewhere. For detailed processing of collection evaluation, one can refer to pages 25–55 in here: https://www.tsl.texas.gov/sites/default/files/public/tslac/ld/ld/pubs/crew /crewmethod12.pdf.

If budget permits, another method is to compare a library's collection with the collection of other libraries using a vendor's research services such as the OCLC WorldShare Collection Evaluation (http://www.oclc.org/collection -evaluation.en.html). These services compare the status of a library's collection with peer institutions and the data found can be used for the deselection and acquisition of collections, as well as for meeting the library's state or institutional accreditation requirements.

CONCLUSION

This book concluded with data collection, user needs analysis, and evaluation and assessment techniques. Data are used to show the evidence of the impact a rural or small library has on its communities. This evidence of practice, the measured outcomes and impacts of practice, is derived from systematically measured, primarily user-based data (Todd, 2015). While it is important to collect information for reports from census data, open library reports, library automation systems, and surveys and interviews, librarians should keep in mind that it is more important to focus on the question to be asked: are the data to be collected for user needs assessment for library outreach programming, or for demonstrating the effects of a library's user services and its impact?

The techniques introduced in this book, such as community outreach, serving diverse users, gaining wide community support, programming dynamic events, and planning rewarding technology learning spaces in libraries, are tools for rural and small libraries to constantly demonstrate their value and impact on their diverse users, outreach partners, governing bodies, and communities a whole, so these libraries can be continuously supported and can become essential components in their communities.

REFERENCES

Agosto, D. E., & Abbas, J. (2011). Teens, social networking, and safety and privacy issues. In D. E. Agosto & J. Abbas (Eds.), *Teens, libraries, and social networking: What librarians need to know* (pp. 59–75). Santa Barbara, CA: ABC-CLIO.

American Library Association. (2013). 2013 state of America's libraries. *American Libraries* [Special issue], 39–44. Available at http://www.ala.org/news/sites/ala.org.news/files/content/2013-State-of-Americas-Libraries-Report.pdf

Barnes, S. B. (2006). A privacy paradox: Social networking in the United States. *First Monday, 11*(9). Available at http://firstmonday.org/ojs/index.php/fm/article/viewArticle/1394/1312%2523

Blake, B., Marin, R., & Du, Y. (2011). *Successful community outreach: A how-to-do-it manual for librarians*. Chicago, IL: ALA.

Case, D. O. (2012). *Looking for information: A survey of research on information seeking, needs, and behavior* (3rd ed.). Bingley, United Kingdom: Emerald Group.

Charbonneau, D. H. (2007). *Demystifying survey research: Practical suggestions for effective question design*. Detroit, MI: Wayne State University. Available at http://digitalcommons.wayne.edu/cgi/viewcontent.cgi?article=1000&context=libsp

Connaway, L. S., & Powell, R. R. (2010). *Basic research methods for librarians*. Santa Barbara, CA: Libraries Unlimited.

Dankowski, T. (2013). How libraries are using social media. *American Libraries, 44*(5), 38–41. Available at http://americanlibrariesmagazine.org/2013/07/16/how-libraries-are-using-social-media/

Dowd, N. (2013). Social media: Libraries are posting, but is anyone listening? [Web log post]. *Library Journal*. Available at http://lj.libraryjournal.com/2013/05/marketing/social-media-libraries-are-posting-but-is-anyone-listening

Downing, M., Brown, V., & Colletti, C. (n.d.). What is environmental scanning? Springfield, IL: Illinois State Library. Available at https://cyberdriveillinois.com/departments/library/grants/pdfs/environmental_scanning.pdf

Eggert, C. (2014). Library surveys for success. *WebJunction Course Catalog*. Available at http://learn.webjunction.org/course/search.php?search=library+surveys+for+success

Hernon, P. (2000). Survey research: Time for some changes. *Journal of Academic Librarianship 26*(2), 83–84.

Larson, G. (2008). *Evaluating your collection: Best practices for North Texas libraries.* Dallas, TX: North Texas Regional Library System. Available at http://www.ntrls .org/ConsultantReports/NTRLS_EvaluatingYourCollection.pdf

Larson, G. (2012). *CREW: A weeding manual for modern libraries.* Austin, TX: Texas State Library and Archives Commission. Available at https://www.tsl.texas.gov/sites /default/files/public/tslac/ld/ld/pubs/crew/crewmethod12.pdf

Library Research Services. (n.d.). Strategies for tracking and reporting Wifi usage. Available at http://www.lrs.org/data-tools/public-libraries/strategies-tracking-reporting -wifi-usage/

Manktelow, J. (n.d.). *SWOT analysis: Discover new opportunities, manage and eliminate threats.* London, United Kingdom: Mind Tools. Available at http://www.mindtools .com/pages/article/newTMC_05.htm

Morrison, J. L. (1992). Environmental scanning. In M. A. Whitely, J. D. Porter, & R. H. Fenske (Eds.), *A primer for new institutional researchers* (pp. 86–99). Tallahassee, FL: The Association for Institutional Research.

Peterson, R. A. (2000). *Constructing effective questionnaires.* Thousand Oaks, CA: Sage.

Social Explorer. (n.d.). About social explorer. New York: Social Explorer. Available at http://www.socialexplorer.com/about

Stueart, R. D., & Moran, B. B. (2007). *Library and information center management.* Santa Barbara, CA: Libraries Unlimited.

Todd, R. (2015). *Evidence-based practice and school libraries, 42*(3), 8–15.

Young Adult Library Services Association. (2011). *Teens & social media in school & public libraries: A toolkit for librarians & library workers.* Chicago, IL: Youth Adult Library Services Association, American Library Association. Available at http://www.ala.org /yalsa/sites/ala.org.yalsa/files/content/professionaltools/Handouts/sn_toolkit11.pdf

SELECTED ANNOTATED BIBLIOGRAPHY WITH BOOKS ON SERVING DIVERSE USERS IN LIBRARIES

AGE DIVERSITY

Crash Course in Library Services for Seniors by Ann Roberts and Stephanie G. Bauman (2012). Libraries Unlimited.

This book provides a refreshingly positive approach to working with older adults—one that focuses on the positive effects of aging on patrons, and the many opportunities that libraries can create for themselves by offering top-notch services delivered with a concierge mindset. The book offers page after page of great programming ideas specifically for reaching out to Baby Boomers and older customers—a population that is predicted to double over the next 20 years.

Crash Course in Teen Services by Donna P. Miller (2007). Libraries Unlimited.

Learn about the world of today's teens and how to communicate with this very important segment of your library's audience. Gather ideas for enlisting help from teachers and school librarians in planning programming to bring teens to the library. Examples of real life reference interviews follow a list of tools to have at the teen reference desk. The essential elements of building teen collection and reader's advisory services are presented with ideas for creating a teen friendly library. Information will be useful to librarians in smaller libraries and persons assigned to teen services as a part of their other duties.

Diversity in Youth Literature: Opening Doors through Reading by Jamie Campbell Naidoo and Sarah Park Dahlen (2013). American Library Association Editions.

The authors show how books have grown to include every area of diversity currently seen in society, including the more familiar topics of racism and sexual orientation, while at the same time addressing lesser-known areas, such as foreign adoption and homelessness. This book also offers tips for librarians and educators when selecting diversity literature in the library and classroom.

Diversity Programming for Digital Youth: Promoting Cultural Competence in the Children's Library by Jamie Campbell Naidoo (2014). Libraries Unlimited.

A guide for selecting the best forms of digital technology for outreach to children, with the purpose of libraries being the fostering an environment for cultural literacy programs and cultural competence amongst children. This book includes outlines of storytime programs that incorporate diverse cultures while utilizing digital technology, as well as interviews with children's librarians who have implemented successful digital programs at their own libraries, in order to engage culturally diverse youth.

Elder Tales: Stories of Wisdom and Courage from Around the World by Dan Keding (2007). Libraries Unlimited.

Traditional folktales from around the world celebrate the wisdom, courage, and even the follies of elders, presenting them as crones, wise men, sages, magic helpers, and fools. Arranged by story type, these are tales that can be used in the classroom and library, as a springboard for cultural comparisons and discussions of how wisdom is shared between generations and how elders contribute to and are perceived by various societies. It is also a fine resource for storytellers performing in senior centers, assisted living facilities, and nursing homes.

DIFFERENTLY DISABLED

Crash Course in Library Services to People with Disabilities by Ann Roberts and Richard J. Smith (2010). Libraries Unlimited.

The authors found that very few librarians feel comfortable with providing services addressed to the needs of the disabled, yet those who do offer services and programs that other libraries can adopt and adapt.

Crash Course in Library Services to People with Disabilities will help librarians get up to speed in understanding disabled persons and understanding what librarians can do to make library premises and holdings more accessible to those who are disabled. This book provides basic information on the different types of mental and physical disabilities a librarian might encounter, then offers a range of exemplary policies, services, and programs for people with disabilities—efforts that are in place and working across the country.

Information Services for People with Developmental Disabilities: The Library Manager's Handbook by Linda Lucas Walling and Marilyn M. Irwin (1995). Libraries Unlimited.

Developmental disabilities are the most numerous of disabilities, and they are exceptionally complex. This professional reference overviews developmental disabilities, discusses the information needs of people with developmental disabilities, and provides practical guidance to librarians and information professionals who serve them. Particular attention is given to the ramifications of the Americans with Disabilities Act for librarians.

Keep It Simple: A Guide to Assistive Technologies by Ravonne A. Green and Vera Blair (2011). Libraries Unlimited.

This book provides a basic tutorial on common assistive computer applications and commonly available, inexpensive hardware and software to help librarians incorporate such aids into the library's current infrastructure. The book offers guidance for the practitioner that can help every library move toward universal access. Librarians will find advice on planning accessible services, selecting appropriate assistive technologies, marketing disability services and assistive technology, and training staff in disability services issues and the use of assistive technology. Individual chapters cover print, hearing, speech, and mobility disabilities, offering resources and tutorials for each of these disability categories.

IMMIGRANTS AND INTERNATIONAL CULTURE

Library Services for Multicultural Patrons: Strategies to Encourage Library Use by Carol Smallwood and Kim Becnel, Editors (2013). The Scarecrow Press.

The book begins with how to organize and find partners, how to reach students, and how to find community connections. It then moves into the "nitty-gritty," with advice on applying new technology, using outreach, programming, and creating events. Best practices for reference services are also shared. Readers of this book will be able to step outside of their cultural identities and adapt these success stories to their current needs.

Serving New Immigrant Communities in the Library by Sondra Cuban (2007). Libraries Unlimited.

Build strong bridges with new members of your community. This book helps to assess current organizational performance with immigrants, gather data, and use that information to gain support for organizational initiatives. It helps to discover how to adapt policies to better fit changing needs, overcome language barriers, develop public relations strategies that reach immigrants, and build culturally relevant collections, services, and programs for a changing community. Filled with quotes, anecdotes, and profiles from the author's research with immigrant communities, the book provides both a positive vision and a practical plan for serving immigrants in your library, school, or organization.

Still Struggling for Equality: American Public Library Services with Minorities by Plummer Alston Jones, Jr. (2004). Libraries Unlimited.

A companion volume to *Immigrants and the American Experience* (1999), this book covers American public library services to immigrants from 1876 to 2003. As such it provides an excellent text on public library services to diverse groups and multiculturalism in public libraries. It presents a detailed exposition of immigration law, accompanied by an analysis of laws affecting libraries. These legislative activities are placed in the context of library practice and the library profession, treating fully developments within the American Library Association (ALA) and the government agencies tasked with the funding and oversight of libraries.

LANGUAGES OR COUNTRY OF ORIGIN

Crash Course in Serving Spanish-Speakers by Salvador Avila (2008). Libraries Unlimited.

This introduction will help plan for attracting this rapidly growing Spanish-speaking population to the library and library services, a major challenge to librarians in small public libraries who have no Spanish-speaking staff.

Providing services to Spanish speakers is both an honor and a challenge. Before public institutions venture into reaching out to the Spanish-speaking community, they need to become familiar with their cultural competency so that their decisions and initiatives are not at risk.

¡Hola, amigos! A Plan for Latino Outreach by Susana G. Baumann (2010). Libraries Unlimited.

This book provides a practical, easy-to-follow guide to creating a bilingual-friendly facility that will attract Latino users. It offers users a systematic, orderly plan that directs outreach activity with worksheets, discussion reports, easy-to-follow schedules, and more than 100 marketing ideas, tips, and examples from libraries around the country that can easily be incorporated into day-to-day activities. Many of the strategies can be applied to outreach of other minorities as well.

Pathways to Progress: Issues and Advances in Latino Librarianship by John L. Ayala and Salvador Güereña, Editors (2011). Libraries Unlimited.

Coverage of library service to the Latino community includes subjects such as special collections, recruitment and mentoring, leadership, collection development, reference services to gays and lesbians, children's services, and special library populations.

Contributors include library practitioners who are of Mexican, Chilean, Peruvian, Nicaraguan, Puerto Rican, and Cuban descent. Best practices are presented and explained in-depth with practical examples and documented citations.

RACE

The 21st-Century Black Librarian in America: Issues and Challenges edited by Andrew P. Jackson, Julius Jefferson Jr., and Akilah S. Nosakhere (2012). Scarecrow Press.

Comprised of 48 essays by black librarians who come from every area of librarianship, including those fresh out of school to those who have retired, this book covers the concerns held by many in the library profession who continue to see the racial divide and its challenges in America. With a great focus on the implementation of technology and information science, within both public as well as school libraries, these essays address the racism seen in the history of libraries, their operations, and the recruitment of black library staff.

Unfinished Business: Race, Equity and Diversity in Library and Information Science Education edited by Maurice B. Wheeler (2004). Scarecrow Press.

Analyzing the evidence that few library and information science programs have truly integrated racial equality in their practice, this book looks at diversity from three angles: faculty and curriculum, student recruitment, and the external and environmental forces at play. While the editors do show where education in this area has fallen short, including issues such as admissions and the financial aid process for students of color, they do approach the idea of the future these programs as being full of promise.

SEXUAL ORIENTATION

Gay, Lesbian, Bisexual, and Transgendered Literature: A Genre Guide by Ellen Bosman, John P. Bradford, and Robert B. Ridinger (2008). Libraries Unlimited.

The book aims to provide the reader and readers' advisor with an introduction to 20th-century gay, lesbian, bisexual, and transgendered literature. All popular genres of literature are examined, including fiction, drama, and life stories (biography, autobiography, and memoirs), with the main emphasis on current fiction. More than 1,100 titles are organized according to genres, subgenres, and formats. Annotations provide brief, engaging plot summaries, information about awards, indication of which populations are addressed (e.g., gay, lesbian, teen), and often suggestions for read-alike books. Subject terms or keywords accompany each entry to enhance access to more read-alike books. A brief history of the literature, comments on the genres, and tips for working with readers make this an essential guide and reference resource.

INDEX

Index

Index

Index

ABOUT THE AUTHOR

Yunfei Du is associate professor at the University of North Texas (UNT), Denton, TX. He is the principal investigator of UNT's Promoting & Enhancing the Advancement of Rural Libraries (PEARL) project, an initiative for 104 rural libraries in Texas on their community outreach plans. He is the author of dozens of journal articles published in top library and information science (LIS) journals such as *Library & Information Science Research* and *Journal of Education for Library and Information Science* and is a coauthor of a book on library community outreach. Du and his colleagues won a 2010 Cutting Edge Award for their paper at the 2010 Academy of Human Resource Development's International Research Conference in the Americas.